WESTCHESTER PUBLIC LIBR

3 1310 00233 3710

W9-BST-730

THIS IS
GONNA
HURT

THIS IS GONNA HURT

The Life of a Mixed Martial Arts Champion

TITO ORTIZ

with Marc Shapiro

SSE

SIMON SPOTLIGHT ENTERTAINMENT
New York London Toronto Sydney

796.8092
Ort

Simon Spotlight Entertainment
A Division of Simon & Schuster, Inc.
1230 Avenue of the Americas
New York, NY 10020

Copyright © 2008 by Tito Ortiz

All rights reserved, including the right to reproduce this book
or portions thereof in any form whatsoever. For information
address Pocket Books Subsidiary Rights Department,
1230 Avenue of the Americas, New York, NY 10020

First Simon Spotlight Entertainment hardcover edition June 2008

SIMON SPOTLIGHT ENTERTAINMENT and colophon are
trademarks of Simon & Schuster, Inc.

For information about special discounts for bulk purchases,
please contact Simon & Schuster Special Sales at
1-800-456-6798 or business@simonandschuster.com

Designed by Gabe Levine

Manufactured in the United States of America

10   9   8   7   6   5   4   3   2   1

Library of Congress Cataloging-in-Publication Data

Ortiz, Tito, 1975–
    This is gonna hurt: the life of a UFC champion / by Tito Ortiz.
        p. cm.
    ISBN-13: 978-1-4169-5541-2 (hardcover)
    ISBN-10:   1-4169-5541-0 (hardcover)
1. Mixed martial arts—Biography.   2. Mixed martial arts.   I. Title.
    GV1101.O77   2008
    796.8092—dc22
    [B]   2008006718

To my son Jacob and all the kids in the world. Dream your dreams and don't let anything get in the way of making your dreams a reality.

TABLE OF CONTENTS

Gimme Some Truth

When I was a kid I had lots of dreams.

I was nine years old and running with some friends who used to sniff glue all the time. In hindsight, it was a dumb thing to do, but back in the day, that's what kids did and I was right there with them when they did it. When I would sniff glue, I would get real high and hallucinate. I would hallucinate that people were all around me, taking my picture and saying, "Tito, look this way! Look this way!" I would look up and see my name on a marquee. In big letters it said: TITO ORTIZ. I had dreams. I had lots of dreams about growing up and being famous. I didn't really know what it meant to be a star when I was nine years old, but just thinking about it made me feel real good at a time when my life was shit.

I remember realizing years later, long after I stopped sniffing glue, got a lot smarter, and began taking the idea of being an Ultimate Fighter seriously, that the dreams had become a reality.

I was defending my Ultimate Fighting Championship belt against Elvis Sinosic in a packed arena in New Jersey. I had defended my title several times over the years, and once I became the top dog on the mixed martial arts scene, I brought fans down on both sides of Tito Ortiz.

Some people hated me and booed me whenever I fought. Some people loved me and cheered. There was no middle ground. But the main thing was that people knew me as the champion. It was my hand that was inevitably raised in victory and it was my opponent's body that usually ended up on the floor at my feet.

I have a high opinion of myself. Call it ego, cockiness, whatever the hell you want. But the reality is that I am the best of the best in a very brutal sport.

At the Sinosic fight, the cheers easily outnumbered the boos as I walked down the stage and into the caged-in Octagon. Flames from my pre-fight entrance shot up toward the ceiling. That night my entrance music was "Ortiz Anthem" by Fieldy's Dreams from the *Rock N Roll Gangster* album, and it was bumping. I entered carrying my trademark American and Mexican flags, the symbols of pride in my mixed heritage. Thousands of people were screaming my name. The lights went out. I was all caught up in the electricity of the moment.

And I started crying.

I had gone from being this little punk kid, whose parents

were heroin addicts and whose mother was seeing men for money, to being here at center stage. All I could think of at that moment was that all these people were here for me. It touched me. I had made it.

I had lots of dreams when I was a kid—a kid whose future looked like a road map of addiction, prison, or death. Now, barely in my mid-twenties, I was living the best possible dream.

Success.

It's been a few years since then—a lot of fights, a lot of ups and downs. I've made it to age thirty-two.

I'm sitting in my home in Huntington Beach, California, getting ready to tell the stories, good and bad, that have made up my life. Writing this book is like therapy for me. And I'll be honest with you, I feel more than a little bit of anxiety at the idea of opening up my life to countless strangers.

People are going to feel things when they read this book. People who thought they knew everything there was to know about me, the people I consider close friends, are going to learn things that they didn't know before. By the time you finish this book, you are going to know everything there is to know about me.

And maybe more than you want to know.

I'm not afraid to say these things, to let people know where I really came from and how I got here. All the material stuff—the cars, the houses, the money—yeah, I have all that and I've worked real hard to get those things. But that's the superficial shit. What's important is to explain how I got to this point . . . and to clear up all the misconceptions.

This book is going to let people know who Tito Ortiz really is.

To the people who pay good money to watch me fight and who read the stories in magazines and on the Internet, I'm known as the big, strong, and, yes, cocky fighter who kicks people's asses for money. The Huntington Beach Bad Boy, a larger-than-life professional hit man who bloodies people and breaks bones.

But for me it really isn't about the fighting. Because I'm not really a fighter. I'm an Aquarius—an Aquarius to a T. I'm a soft-spoken, cool guy with all my friends. Before just about every fight I've ever had, I've cried. A lot of times I've even thrown up. But that was just the fear leaving me.

When it's fight time, I flip the switch on and there's this character that comes out of me that's not me. I have an out-of-body experience when I fight. I see myself fight from a place outside the ring. It sounds like some kind of fantasy. But make no mistake, when I fight it's a brutal reality.

Months and months of training go into that fifteen minutes in the cage. When I'm in the Octagon and I'm repeatedly punching a guy in the face, there are no pulled punches, no screwups, and no thrown matches. At that moment, I'm doing everything in my power to break down my opponent and destroy him.

But then it's over and I go back to being the guy I've always been. I'll go out and party. I'll drink and, although I don't do it much anymore, I might smoke a joint. I'll hang out with my friends and spend some time with my woman. In other words, when the fight's over, I go back to being Tito Ortiz. Regular guy.

This book is not intended to make me out to be some kind of saint or role model. I couldn't be either if I tried. Because I'm flawed. I'm imperfect. I've made mistakes. Lots of them.

By the time I reached the sixth grade, I had done just about every drug there was to do except heroin. I would never do heroin because I saw how it had destroyed my parents' lives and I didn't want to go down that road. But pot? Acid? Mushrooms? Sure, I did it all. Especially when I wasn't drinking. I was a drug dealer for a time, selling marijuana, cocaine, and methamphetamine in order to survive.

I was a tough, streetwise kid who ran with a gang called F Troop, and we did a lot of bad shit. I did two sentences in juvenile detention centers. I almost died twice. And in one of those instances someone I cared deeply about nearly died.

I've been unfaithful too many times to count. Affairs meant nothing to me but momentary sexual gratification. That people were getting hurt in the process meant nothing to me. After all, I was Tito Ortiz, a big kid playing in an adult sandbox and trying to overcome the lack of attention and the abandonment that had haunted me since the day I was born.

The fact that my parents were drug addicts is the one thing that haunts me the most. It hurt, but it also changed my life. If they had not been drug addicts, I might have had a luxurious life. If they had not been drug addicts, what you're about to read might never have happened.

My life has been the worst and it's also been the best.

I've had the love of a good woman named Kristin, who remains an important part of my life as the mother of my son Jacob even though we are no longer together. She is the daily recipient of all the love and respect I can give her. I am in a committed relationship with a wonderful woman named Jenna, whose love and devotion knows no limits. I have made peace with my mother. Sadly, my father and I remain apart, but I have good friends. I am truly blessed.

And yes, there are people out there who hate my guts. They've said horrible things about me. They've said vile things about the people I care for, which really bothers me. But at the end of the day, I don't really have time for the haters.

Being a role model is definitely out of the question for me. The best I can hope for in writing this book is to be an inspiration.

I think I've got the qualifications for that because I've gone through the best and the worst. I was planning to be a teacher when I finished college. I wanted to take kids who were exactly like me and pull them out of the streets and the gangs and away from parents who were drug addicts and give them some idea of a better life. Being a world-class fighter and someone in the public eye has given me the opportunity to make a difference in a lot of kids' lives.

It's impossible to reach them all. Some have slipped through the cracks—like my childhood friend Nacho, who is currently serving twenty-five to life for a crime I was nearly involved in but, because I didn't want to miss wrestling practice, chose not to do. That day I was awfully damned lucky. Or maybe God was just looking out for me.

I'm getting ready to tell the stories that, for better or worse, have made me the person I am today. And I'll have some help.

Memories are often an elusive thing. Perspectives and impressions are like shifts in the wind. A lot of the important moments in my journey came to pass before I was even born. A lot of important moments were lost to me through years of alienation and a refusal to confront my demons. So at points in my story, the three important women in my life, my mother, Joyce Robles, my ex-wife, Kristin Ortiz, and the love of my life, Jenna Jameson, will fill in the blanks and help paint a complete picture.

Because, in a sense, this is their story as well as mine.

I'm secure. I'm happy. I sleep well at night and I work real hard for my family and the people I love. Those are the things that make Tito Ortiz tick.

I've had a lot of people tell me that I'm living in hell, so I'm surely going to heaven when I die. I'll leave that decision in the hands of God.

Because I know I've done my job as a man on this earth.

CHAPTER ONE

What Did You Call My Mother?

I grew up in Huntington Beach, California.

When you think about that city, certain impressions come to mind. And one of the most popular is surfing in the sixties. White kids surfing. But it wasn't only white kids, even though that's what the Beach Boys would have you believe. Believe it or not, Mexicans surfed too. And fished. And hung out at the beach. And drank beer or smoked a joint with friends if there were no parents around.

If you were a Mexican kid growing up in Huntington Beach, this is what you did.

My father was Mexican. My mother was Anglo. They liked the water, too. I remember my parents this way . . .

My father's name is Samuel Ortiz. He was born in Santa Ana, California, in 1944. His family was also originally from Santa Ana, although the Ortiz family did come here from Mexico at some point. Names, dates, and places are hard to remember, but my father would tell me stories when I was younger. He was in the army in the sixties. He ran with local gangs a bit when he was growing up, but mostly he hung out with car clubs like the Night Owls, who would cruise around Santa Ana in their tricked-out cars.

My father graduated from high school, but he did not go to college. He started out as a carpenter and worked as a contractor before forming his own company. He was a successful craftsman and a great artist.

JOYCE ROBLES   *He made a lot of the family's clothes. He was a designer, an artist. He was totally outrageous.*

My mother's name is Joyce Robles. Before that she was Joyce Johnson. Before that she was Joyce Simmons. She was born on the island of Hawaii, in Hilo, in 1948.

JOYCE ROBLES   *My father was a missionary. We would travel a lot. Some days we would have these tent services. On other days we would stand on street corners, swinging our tamborines. We were doing our Pentacostal thing, just trying to bring in the sinners.*

My mother was the oldest of six sisters. Her father, Herman, served in World War II. Her mother, whom I've only ever referred to as Grandma, died when I was nine years old.

JOYCE ROBLES   *My parents would always say that one day* *we would go to the mainland. Which meant California. Which meant Long Beach. We moved there in 1965.*

My mother did not go to high school. Things were tight, moneywise, for a family with six kids, so my mother stayed home to take care of her sisters while her parents worked. She did it grudgingly. I remember conversations with my mother where she said that her dad was hard on her when she was growing up.

Maybe that's why she married her first husband at such a young age.

JOYCE ROBLES *I met Louie Simmons when I was fourteen years old. He was a friend of a friend. By the time I was fifteen we were a couple.*

Her first husband's name was Louie Simmons. I met him once, but I don't really know much about him. She was with him for eight years and had three kids with him, all boys. Jimmy, Mike, and Marty, each born three years apart.

JOYCE ROBLES *Louie and I got married really young. I was seventeen when I had our first son, Jim. We were very loving in the beginning. But then things got tough. He was always wanting to go out to the nightclubs and act crazy. I wouldn't go to the nightclubs because I was a good missionary girl. So I stayed home and tried to be Donna Reed. Louie Simmons was a cheater and a half. I left* *him in late 1971 when our third child, Marty, was eleven months old. We divorced in 1972.*

That's when she found my father.

JOYCE ROBLES *After I divorced Louie, I moved in with my sister Shirley and later moved out with a friend of mine to a place in Huntington Beach. One day I was on an outing with the kids in Newport Beach when I met Tito's father. He saw my little boys and he knew they didn't have a daddy with them. But that didn't seem to bother him. Two months later we went on a date and after that we were like glue. He was a very handsome man. A mixture of Carlos Santana and Jerry Garcia of the Grateful Dead.*

My mom and dad's courtship was simply a matter of my dad sweeping my mom off her feet. He was a good-looking guy and he was very nice to her. They started going out and one thing led to another and they became a couple.

They began living together in 1974. They were never married on paper—it was like a common-law relationship. They were very loving to each other. My father never cheated on my mother and he never beat her.

In 1974, my father went to prison for eleven months. It went down like this . . .

He and some of his friends were driving to a rock concert. They had some pills and some dime bags of pot in the car. The police pulled them over, took one look at my father with his wild hair and crazy looks, and thought that the weed belonged to him and that he was a dealer. The weed wasn't his and he wasn't dealing, but he was found guilty and did his time.

The first house my parents lived in was this real nice place in Huntington Beach. They stayed there for a while and then they moved to Santa Ana. My mother got pregnant and she had a baby boy. They named him Cesar Sebastian Ortiz. They were ready to stop having children at that point, but Cesar died of SIDS when he was four months old.

JOYCE ROBLES *When Cesar died, we were not thinking about having another child. I was in shock. It was hard to get through the day. For a while I would go to the cemetery where Cesar was buried and it would mess me up for weeks afterward. After a while I just stopped going. All of a sudden I got pregnant again. It was like God had sent me an angel.*

If Cesar had lived, I never would have been born. But after Cesar died, my parents wanted to have a kid together so badly that they tried again.

I was born Jacob Christopher Ortiz on January 23, 1975.

My dad was six foot five and my mom was five foot seven, and I was a very big kid. I weighed eleven pounds, eight ounces at birth, and by age one, I weighed forty-five pounds. I wasn't fat; I was just this husky kid. When my mom held me, I measured from her kneecaps to the top of her head.

My father gave me the nickname of Tito when I was about a year old. Tito translated into "tyrant," and it kind of fit because even at age one I was a very bold and bratty kid. But it was apparently mostly in a good way.

My mom would always tell me that everybody always wanted to be around me and talk to me because I constantly gave off this positive kind of energy.

I had a typical relationship with my older brothers. They would beat me up and then turn right around and take care of me. Jim was eleven years older, and he seemed to be the one who would always look out for me. Mike would always tease me and mess with me, and Marty used to beat the shit out of me all the time.

As the youngest, it always seemed like somebody was doing something outrageous to me. Like the time my brother Mike and I were playing on the roof of the house. He thought it would be funny to tie me to the chimney with duct tape and leave me there. I was scared and started screaming. I must have been up there screaming for two hours before my aunt Linda heard me and came to the rescue.

We led a pretty idyllic life. We were living at the beach. My father went to work every day and my mother was a stay-at-home mom, taking care of us kids. As I got older, my brothers and I would spend a lot of days walking down the alleys behind our house to the beach. I used to go swimming and do a little boogie boarding. We would go lay out in the sand and play like regular kids.

Sometimes we'd bring a football and every once in a while one of us would throw the football at somebody's stuff while they were in the water. When we went to retrieve it, we'd grab people's wallets so we'd have money to buy stuff.

I was too young to know that what I was doing was a crime. It just seemed like another fun thing to do.

We were always going on family trips. We'd go to Disneyland and places like Casper Park and Lake Elsinore, where we did a lot of camping and fishing. We liked being outdoors. One time we drove up to Pismo Beach, which is up the California coast, in our VW bus; this was when you could still drive your cars on the beach. We went out there and our van got stuck in the sand and we ended up waiting there until late at night when a bunch of bikers came by and helped pull us out. Those were the good times.

JOYCE ROBLES *The holidays were always special. I remember one year Tito's father spent weeks fixing up the backyard for Halloween. One year the entire family piled into the car and went to this place where there was this old broken-down coffin. We grabbed the coffin for our Halloween party while the kids looked out for the police. There was a very welcoming attitude in our house. All the neighborhood kids hung out there. Tito's father made the kids a tree house. He was always good*

to my children. But for him, Tito was like his
magic child. He truly loved him.

Even though they were not his biological kids, my father took in my mother's children and basically treated them as his own. And for the most part, my half brothers treated him with respect. There were the arguments, but for the most part things were settled peacefully. Except for the time my brother Mike, who was always a little crazy anyway, got mad at my father and tried to set him on fire.

My dad had gotten into it with Mike for some reason. When it was over my dad went to bed. But Mike was still pissed. So he snuck into my dad's bedroom, splashed some lighter fluid on him, and threw a lit match at him. My dad jumped up and put the fire out before he was seriously burned. Mike got a serious whipping for pulling that stunt.

At one time or another we all acted out and got punished. I remember getting whipped with a belt once because I stole some money from one of my father's friends. Whenever we would get a whipping, it wasn't about abuse, it was about us learning. And I definitely learned not to steal money from my dad's friends.

Dad and I used to go hunting quite a bit, and he would let me shoot guns even though I was still a tiny kid. I remember one day we were out hunting and my dad let me fire a twelve-gauge shotgun. I fired and the kickback from the shotgun knocked me on my ass and I started crying. My mom was pissed off when she found out.

"Why in the hell did you let him shoot a shotgun?" she yelled at my dad.

But I got into plenty of trouble on my own. I was kind of a smart-ass even at a young age. There was the day that I almost set the backyard on fire. A bunch of cut grass had dried and had been piling up for a couple of weeks. I stacked up all the grass and started flicking lit matches at it. The pile caught fire just about the time my mom came home. She yelled at me and gave me the "Wait until your father gets home" speech. My dad came home and I got a good ass-whipping.

Sometimes it seemed like we got hit a lot. But my parents never really beat us.

We would get a whipping if we got out of line, but it was never anything serious. It was more of a serious scolding than anything else. I remember my mom slapping me in the head a couple of times when I was younger. While I'm not in favor of physical abuse of any kind, I do believe that a good whipping once in a while helps keep a kid in line. So I believe my parents were right in what they were doing.

I started preschool at age five at Eader Elementary, which was at the intersection of Pacific Coast Highway and Magnolia in Huntington Beach. My parents were kind of into the hippie thing back then, so haircuts were not a big priority. Consequently I had hair down to my ass on that first day of school.

The other kids jumped on that and began making fun of me. They would say things like, "There was a little girl and his name was Jacob." I remember coming home crying and telling my mom. She said, "Well, I guess we'll just have to cut your hair." So they did and I ended up with a Mohawk. That worked out pretty well for the weekend, but by the time I went back to school the next week, my head was completely shaved.

And then I was teased for being bald. Kids can be pretty cruel even at that young age. But for the most part I got along pretty well with everyone. I was a leader in school, probably due to a combination of my size and attitude. I wasn't afraid of anything, and if I told somebody to do something, they usually did it. Sometimes there would be problems with the other kids. One day I was playing on the playground slide and one of the kids called my mom a bitch.

"What did you say?" I remember saying.

"I said your mother is a bitch," he answered.

Well, I got real mad and pushed the kid off the swing he was on and made him cry. I got in trouble for that. The teacher wanted to know what happened, but I wouldn't tell on the guy. There was a code even at that young age that you did not snitch on anybody.

I told the teacher that he was talking about my mom, but I wouldn't tell anybody what he said. My mom got called to the school to pick me up and she wanted to know what happened. I said, "This guy called you a fucking bitch." She told me to watch my mouth. I cussed a lot back then and the teachers would always wash my mouth out with soap.

Then there were the drugs.

My parents smoked pot. It was part of that seventies hippie thing that was going on at the time. My dad and mom
grew up in the sixties and they always used drugs. They were
real stoners. In fact, there was an issue of *Time* magazine in
the 1970s that covered this big outdoor California rock festival called the US Festival. And if you look real closely at one
of the pictures, you can see my dad with his big Afro and he
sure looked like he was having a good time.

They would smoke with their friends at parties and after
work. It wasn't an addiction so much as a lifestyle; it wasn't
hurting their day-to-day lives. Dad would always get high,
but he was able to go off to work each day and do his job.
Mom was always good about getting us up and making sure
our clothes were clean, we were fed, and our needs were
taken care of. We would always see them smoking. It didn't
mean a whole lot to me at the time. It was just something my
parents and their friends did, and it always seemed to make
them mellow.

JOYCE ROBLES *Sam and I were hippies. Stone hippies. Marijuana
was a very big part of our lifestyle. It was all
about the herb. The kids had things to do so they
weren't sitting around watching us smoke all day.
When Tito was real young, a couple of years old,
he was not aware of our lifestyle. But when he got
a little older, he knew it was a natural thing in
the home. He was a very wise boy.*

The reason my parents' smoking pot was not a big deal

to me was because my brothers used to smoke pot and they turned me on to it when I was five years old. Getting high at age five was not so great. I would remember getting head spins that would knock me over and I would have these real bad headaches afterward. It sucked. It just didn't feel good. I also started drinking beer at age five.

JOYCE ROBLES   *I wasn't aware that Tito was doing drugs and drinking that young. If I had known, I would have done something about it.*

My parents weren't concerned because they didn't know we were doing it. They never knew about it at all. We always got away with it, though I never thought about it in those terms. Maybe it was because I was so young. I just felt like they were doing their thing and I was doing mine.

Everybody was getting high and loaded. It was a carefree life.

CHAPTER TWO

Daddy's Not Right, Mommy's Not Right

What my parents went through in the sixties with drugs was kind of what my brothers and I were going through in the eighties. We grew up in the punk rock days. The music and the lifestyle were huge in Santa Ana and Huntington Beach. There were these record stores all over the place, and bands were playing in clubs and in people's backyards. Punk rock was not about peace and love, as our seventies childhoods had been.

The punk thing was very much about rebellion and aggression, something that kids in our neighborhood could relate to. Everybody was into the scene. The music was wild and crazy and had a message that kids were into. Drugs and booze were a big part of that scene. It was all about getting high, being into the music, and partying. But it was still the mellow stuff, pretty much pot and beer for me. I had no idea about things like heroin.

Until my parents started mainlining.

But for my parents, getting into heroin and ultimately becoming addicts was a gradual thing. And not by design. At least not at first. In fact, I guess you could say that my parents became addicts by a simple twist of fate.

It was around 1982 that my father had a cyst removed from his tailbone. He was in a lot of pain after the operation, and the drugs the doctors were giving him weren't easing his pain.

JOYCE ROBLES *While Sam was in the hospital, he came down with pneumonia. At that point the doctors gave him morphine, and when he came out of the hospital, he was so strung out, he couldn't sleep or do anything. So he called his brother Reuben.*

One day my uncle Reuben came over and said, "Try some of this stuff. This will take away the pain."

What he gave my father was heroin.

My father tried it. It worked on his pain. But he also got hooked pretty quickly. Then he turned my mom on to it. I don't know if they were hesitant to try it at first. After all, this was 1982 and nobody really knew how addictive that stuff was.

JOYCE ROBLES *I was in love with Tito's father. If he had said let's jump off the Empire State Building I would have done it. So when he started snorting heroin, I started doing it as well.*

Pretty soon my father and mother were both hooked. And things began to change.

All of a sudden I noticed things going missing around the house, things like TVs, and I soon figured out that my parents had to be selling our possessions to get money for the drugs. Then there was no food in the house. Things got so bad that we'd sometimes go through people's trash cans to try and find something to eat. And when we did have a few bucks for food, we would always eat things like beans, rice, and tacos. But mostly any money my parents had was going toward feeding their habit. It wasn't long before I realized that they seemed to be high all the time.

JOYCE ROBLES *At first the kids didn't notice the change. We would still go camping and go out on fishing boats and continue to do normal family kinds of things. The only difference was that we would make sure we brought some junk with us. We would be on a fishing boat, and we'd sneak into a bathroom to do the heroin and then we'd be able to get through the rest of the day without any problem.*

My parents had started out just smoking it. But they began hanging out with people who were mainlining it and pretty soon they were mainlining it too.

Heroin had become a big part of their lives and so it became a big part of their kids' lives as well.

Dad and Mom didn't even try to hide their drug use from

us. I knew when they were doing drugs because there was always the smell of matches. When I smelled the matches I could tell my parents were cooking up the drug, which is why, to this day, the smell of burning matches makes me very sick.

It had reached a point where watching them shoot up became a part of my daily life. After school or playing outside, I would walk in on them and they would quickly hide their works and try to act like nothing was going on. But I knew. There were times when they were getting high right in front of me; the only thing that separated us was a curtain.

I remember looking at that curtain and seeing the outlines of the spoon and the needle as their habit grew worse.

My father stopped showing up for work. He had gone from having a full-time job to just doing occasional odd jobs—a couple of weeks here, a couple of weeks there. He was doing just about anything he could to bring in money to feed their habit while my mother continued to stay home.

JOYCE ROBLES *Anything we had of value in the house would be sold for drug money. At first Tito's father would steal things from work to sell. Eventually things got so bad that he ended up selling his business. It reached the point where he was so hooked that he would just lay in bed for days. And besides, he didn't have the guts to do any big things to get money. So I was the one who kept a roof over our heads. I was the one who would go out and steal* *stuff from stores and then take it back and try to get a refund. At that point everything we did was on the sly. We did not want the neighbors to know, so we did whatever we had to do to hide it.*

By the end of the first year of their addiction, it had gotten so bad at home that I did not want to be around my parents at all. Especially when they were high, which seemed to be all the time. I would come home from school and as soon as they came home I would leave and go hang out with my friends or just wander around the streets.

My parents didn't care. As long as I was home before the streetlights went out in the morning, they were fine with me being gone. I tried to stay away from them and what they were doing as much as possible and tried to lead as normal a life as I possibly could.

I was always getting into mischief, nothing real heavy, just kid stuff. Sometimes it would involve drugs. One time I snuck out of the house and went down the street with a friend to a place that had pot plants growing in the yard. In our neighborhood at that time, drugs had become a part of a lot of people's lifestyles and so it was not uncommon for people to have pot plants growing in their yards. And no one was trying to hide them either. My friend and I decided we were going to steal the plants.

So we went to this house, jumped over the fence, hacksawed the plants off, threw the two big bushes over the fence, and took off. As we were going home, we were trying to decide where we were going to hide the plants. Then I looked up and saw my dad walking down the street toward us. He looked pissed.

"Tito, get your ass over here right now!" he yelled at me.

I was kind of scared. I didn't know what to say. So I held out one of the pot plants.

"Dad, look what I got for you," I said. He wasn't mad anymore.

One time my brothers Mike and Marty and this friend of ours named Larkin found out that this house in Lake Elsinore had these huge pot plants growing. So we drove all the way up to Lake Elsinore, snuck into the yard, chopped down this huge plant, put it in a tarp, and drove with it all the way to Huntington Beach.

All the way back, we were praying that we wouldn't get stopped by the police. When we got back, we all took some of it. I gave some to my mom and dad, who were stoked, and then ended up selling some to a friend of mine. I was supposed to get twenty bucks for it. But he only had ten so I let him slide.

I guess you could say that was the first time I did a drug deal.

The obvious sign that my parents were full-blown addicts was that they barely smoked pot anymore. They used to smoke around us all the time and there would always be weed laying out all around the house. But now it was mostly heroin. And heroin cost a lot of money.

Since all the money we had was being spent on drugs

or, if we were lucky, food, my parents never had money to pay the rent. We started moving from place to place on a fairly regular basis. We must have moved at least four times by the time I turned seven. We would get into a place, fall behind on the rent, get kicked out, move to another place, have enough for the first month's rent, and then the same thing would happen again.

And because we were moving around so much, I was always in and out of different schools. By the time I reached the second grade, I had been in and out of Keppler, Smith, and Wilson in Santa Ana. Actually, I got kicked out of two of those schools for not showing up.

I was feeling so insecure and sad about what was going on with my parents that I basically had no interest in going. A lot of times I would leave for school, decide I wasn't going to go, and end up jumping on a bus that would take me down to Newport Beach, where I would spend the day fishing.

Shortly after I turned six, my three older brothers went to live with this guy named Walter Blanchard. It had become impossible for my parents to support all of us kids. Walter Blanchard was not any relation to us. He was like a friend of a friend who said he'd take my brothers in and watch them while my parents did what they had to do to get to where they needed to be. He knew what was going on. By that time a lot of people did.

The thing with Walter Blanchard was not done legally. It was as simple as my parents approaching him and asking, "Can you do us a favor and watch our sons?" Over the next few years, I would get together with my brothers for birthdays and holidays like Christmas and Thanksgiving. It was fun seeing them when we got together, but I really didn't have any feelings of loss when my brothers left. I just felt that I wanted to be with my mom and dad.

JOYCE ROBLES *Tito was my baby. That was the only reason I kept him with me when the other kids went to live elsewhere.*

By the time I reached age seven, my parents were always fighting about money or some shit about drugs. They could have cared less about what was going on in their kids' lives and we felt it. One night I heard them screaming at each other and I was like, "Gosh! I wish they'd stop fighting!"

Then all of a sudden I heard this loud bang.

Not too long before, my mom had gotten a car from my grandpa, an old Buick. My dad had parked it on the street by our house in this really dark area. That night when my dad heard the bang, he yelled, "What the fuck!" and looked out the front door.

The Buick grandpa had given us was all the way up on the driveway, and a Mustang had crashed into it from behind. This guy staggered out of the Mustang, all bloody from head to toe and totally hammered, and took off running. My dad was so pissed off that he ran after him, grabbed him, and brought him back to our house, where he held him until the police arrived. The guy was arrested for drunk driving and for totaling our car.

My parents got some money from the accident and they went right out and spent it on drugs. But the relative peace of their newly funded high didn't last very long. Pretty soon they would be screaming and hollering about money again. They were running out of ways to feed their habit.

Sadly, my father came up with one more idea.

CHAPTER THREE
Street Life

I've always been a person who speaks his mind. Ask me any question and I'll give you an answer. As far as I'm concerned, nothing is off-limits.

But there's one thing about my life that really touches me and it's something that not many people know about. I am kind of reluctant to talk about it. But I don't feel as though people will truly understand what I've gone through in my life unless they hear this too. So here it is . . .

My mother became a lady of the evening when I was eight years old.

My father was barely working and wasn't bringing in much money. So he and my mother started talking about her going with men for money and eventually my father pushed her into it. My mother never wanted to become that kind of woman. But at the time, for them, it seemed like there was no other way to support their drug habit.

JOYCE ROBLES *I know I made a lot of bad decisions, but I never slept with men for money. I would go with men, play games with them, and then rip them off. But as far as laying down with men for money? No. I ripped them off. They left with no money but they left without me too.*

It started gradually at first, but it would get worse. I remember I would be at home and I would look outside and my mother would be waiting for guys to come and pick her up. I pretty much knew what was going on, and it was painful for me to watch.

JOYCE ROBLES *Of course Tito knew what was going on. I'm sure in his mind, he had to know. He worried about where I would go at night and where I was coming up with all the money.*

There were times when I just had to get away from the situation and I would go down to Newport and fish. Sometimes I would be fishing on the pier and a car would pull up and it would be my mom with some guy. She would take me to someone's house and I would stay there until she was finished, and then she would come and pick me up.

The way it worked was she would come home after being with a customer at night and would give me money to go get some food. I usually went to the Mexican restaurant that was about five blocks away from the house. Then, with whatever money was left, she would get her drugs and get high.

I know my mother hated what she was doing. She hated every second of it. But she also knew that the money she was making was supporting her and my father's drug habit. My father didn't feel any jealousy or anything about pushing her into that kind of life. None at all. All he cared about was getting the money and getting high.

I found out years later that when my mother went with men, she would act like she was somebody else. She would play out a fantasy in her head so she could escape the reality of what she was doing.

My mother had some run-ins with the law, but she was never in jail for more than a night. My father never went back to jail. Considering the shit he was doing, I guess you would have to say he was lucky.

But the one thing about my parents, even with all the shit that was going on with them, was that they still insisted that I go to school. Nobody in school—not friends, not teachers, nobody—knew what my life was like. They didn't have a clue because I wouldn't talk about it.

Kind of like what my mother was doing when she was with men, I was living a fantasy when I was in school. When I went to school, I would think that I was just like any other kid. My mom would pick me up and drop me off. A lot of times I would just walk.

I was pretty much a C student. I had a lot of problems with English classes even though my parents were strictly English-speaking and that's what was spoken in the house. I had problems reading. My favorite subjects were geography, science, and math. But learning was tough for me. Between the second and fourth grades, I never went to school for a full year. But I made it to enough classes and got good enough grades that somehow they passed me.

Sometimes I would get suspended because I acted out, looking for the attention I wasn't getting at home. I would start fights, sit in the back of the class and throw things, stuff like that.

When I wasn't in school, I was stealing. I would go to places like Kmart and steal clothes and food. I had picked up on my parents' habits. Stealing was the only skill I had. When we didn't have the money to buy things, we would steal them.

I really didn't want to spend time at home—except when it was time to watch pro wrestling on television. My mom told me that when I was young, I would come into the house, get completely naked, grab my blanket, and sit in front of the television watching wrestling. I was fascinated by it. I loved Hulk Hogan and all the trash talking and, of course, the action. I was convinced that it was all real. My mother once told me that I turned to her one day and told her that my name was going to be up in lights someday. I guess that's when the dream was born.

It was about this time that my parents were finding it impossible to keep a roof over our heads and we basically became nomads. Between the ages of eight and nine, I remember staying in a lot of motels, places like Motel 6 and Best Western. When we couldn't afford a motel we'd sleep in our car. For a time we had this tiny trailer that we would park in people's backyards and stay there. Sometimes we would stay in people's garages.

JOYCE ROBLES *We lived in a trailer for a while that was next to a campground. Haitian gypsies were living right next door. One day Tito came running up to the trailer and told us that there were narcs in the front yard. We all ran out of the trailer, jumped a fence, and ran to a friend's house to hide.*

I had friends, but I always made some kind of excuse as to why they couldn't come over to my house. I was ashamed and embarrassed to have them see that I was living in a motel or in somebody's garage.

We used to get food stamps and government cheese and milk. We were on that whole government-issue deal. On Christmas, we'd go and have Christmas dinner with home-less people. That was my memory of Christmas for a lot of years. It was all pretty sad.

I had been getting high for a long time, but I was eight when I started getting heavily into shit. I was hanging out with these guys who were always looking for ways to get high. I started off sniffing paint and glue, but eventually we did whatever we could get our hands on. I wasn't in a gang, but I was definitely hanging out with some tough street guys.

Things were bad, but I can remember some bright spots.

Every once in a while my father would take me out on a fishing boat called the *Hellena* with his friends. We had done a lot of fishing before, and it had become my thing. I would read about fishing a lot. We would be out on the ocean catching fish and as they were pulling them in, I would be able to call out their names. One of the deckhands, a guy named Mark Thompson, said, "How do you know about those fish?" When I told him I read about them, he was real impressed.

"Have you ever thought about working on a boat?" he asked me one day.

I told him I hadn't.

He said, "Why don't you come out and I'll show you a few things. You can scrub the boat down and I'll let you fish for free."

That sounded cool to me. So every chance I had, I would go down to Newport Landing. My mom would drop me off, I would work on the boat, and my mom would pick me up at night. For me it was a total getaway. It was a few hours where I didn't have to see my parents doing drugs.

My mother did her best. She tried. But to this day, I still have hatred toward my father.

I hate him for what he put us through and because he could never be man enough to talk to me about it. But when my dad wasn't high on drugs, he could be very loving toward me.

I remember the times when I would lay on his chest

and we would watch television and just talk about things. I remember his smell and his hairy chest. At that time, those things were very comforting to me. There was a little happiness for me with my parents.

They had good hearts.

CHAPTER FOUR

F Troop

*M*y family had just made our latest move to a house on the corner of McFadden and Bristol in Santa Ana. Nothing had changed. My parents were still doing drugs and doing whatever they had to do to get the money for the drugs. And because of that I was spending a lot of time on the streets.

The first time I got into a one-on-one street fight I was twelve years old.

It was in Garden Grove, California, and I fought against some Asian kid. I don't remember his name. But I remember that the whole thing was as simple as him saying something about one of my friends and my sticking up for him. We were standing face-to-face and then all of a sudden he slapped me real hard in the ear. I started crying and I ran home.

I learned something that day. You've got to watch out for those ear punches.

I never went back to try and even the score with that guy because I was scared to death of him.

Not too long after that, I got into my second one-on-one fight. There was this kid who was trying to bully me. I stood up to him and punched him real hard. He fell down, started crying, and ran away. He never bullied me again.

That kind of evened the score.

By the time I had those fights, I had already been jumped in and jumped out of one of the toughest gangs in the Santa Ana area. They were the baddest of the bad. They were F Troop.

I didn't really know who was who at first. There were just a bunch of guys hanging out and getting into shit. Most days I was hanging out on the streets with a lot of the neighborhood kids, and some of the older kids, the guys fourteen to sixteen, were in gangs. I was nine at the time but I was pretty mature and streetwise for my age, so people thought I was a lot older.

Most of the guys I was hanging with were members of F Troop. Even before I actually knew anybody in the gang, I knew what they were about. I heard all the stories, how they were the in crowd at the time. Those were the people I wanted to be around. They were one of the biggest gangs in Santa Ana.

It wasn't like I asked to be in F Troop, and they didn't exactly approach me to join the gang. I had been hanging out with some of the members for a while and they basically said that if I wanted to keep hanging out with them, I had to join the gang. So finally they asked, "Do you want to get jumped in?" And when I said yeah, they said, "Okay, tomorrow we're going to meet here and you'd better be here." I looked at it as a friends kind of thing and wasn't really afraid.

Being jumped in is an initiation beating. You have to walk this line of about eight kids, usually four on a side. As you walk the line they all beat on you and sucker punch you and you have to take it to prove you're strong enough to join their gang. At the end of this line there's always one guy who gives you the final beatdown.

At first, I wasn't really afraid—I didn't give it much thought. But all of a sudden, that night, I started getting scared. I wasn't sure if they were going to shoot me or stab me.

According to the rules, I basically had to let them beat the shit out of me and I could not fight back. But I kind of got the feeling that they would look up to me if I did fight back. So I started walking the line and as I was getting hit with all kinds of punches, I started getting angry about half-way down the line. I knew if I didn't put up a fight, these guys were going to beat the shit out of me. So I started trying to defend myself a little bit and I hit a couple of guys pretty hard. I reached the end of the line and the beating stopped. I had a bloody lip and a swollen eye, and they told me I was part of the family now.

I liked the idea of the family thing. My parents knew nothing about F Troop or what I had been doing with them. They were too busy getting high all the time to care about me. So it was like F Troop had become my family.

JOYCE ROBLES *I had no idea that Tito had joined that gang. It was all a secret. I wasn't all there in my mind so I really didn't know. When I did find out later, the idea that he was in a gang scared me to death.*

F Troop was always into some kind of bad shit in the neighborhood, and I got right into the swing of things. We would tag and spray paint on walls. We did a lot of drugs. I did pot a lot and PCP a couple of times and, of course, I drank. F Troop was also into stealing things to get the money to buy drugs and stuff.

Sadly, given my background, I was pretty good at stealing. I would steal stereos from cars that we'd break into, or we'd go into stores as a group and walk out with car stereos, candy, and alcohol. It wasn't like we were stealing and then trying to sell the stuff. We would take orders from people wanting certain things.

Stealing was easy for me because nobody really paid any attention to a small kid. Once in a while we would get caught, but we would just get a slap on the hand and then they'd kick us out of the store.

There was a lot of violence in and around F Troop. But it never seemed to go beyond just beating the shit out of people. A lot of the violence was gang-on-gang action. If other gangs were on our turf, we'd beat them up. That happened a lot in Centennial Park, where we hung out. It was pretty much our turf. One day we came across three members of a rival gang there, so we just beat the crap out of them. That they were there was all it took to justify a beat-down.

There was no technique involved in gang fighting. You would just sling, throw blows, punches, kicks, and tackles. Sometimes we would use baseball bats and chains. All we wanted to do was hurt them, beat them down, and make them cry.

But I never used a gun or a knife. I never killed anybody or beat anybody real seriously. There were a couple of times when F Troop wanted to use guns, but I said no way. I was afraid; using guns and knives was way too serious for me. But I was more than up for throwing blows.

When I was in F Troop, there was always the chance of things getting out of hand and going too far. I could have ended up in jail or worse. I was an angry kid, but it was a controlled anger. I believed in what my gang stood for, and the guys were friends and family to me. So yeah, while I was definitely an angry kid, it was never an anger that was going to get me into real serious trouble as long as I was careful.

But the funny thing was that even though I was into a lot of shit with F Troop, I knew the stuff I was doing wasn't good. Something in my heart was telling me that I wasn't being a good person.

This went on for another two years until I was about twelve. And the funny thing was, by that time, I was probably doing more drugs than my parents were.

It still both angered and saddened me that they were heroin addicts. But there was really nothing I could do.

Although I would sometimes try. I remember sneaking into the house sometimes when they weren't home and hiding their works. But then my father would come home and get real angry when he couldn't find them. When he asked me, I flat out told him that I had hidden them so they couldn't do drugs anymore. But all that did was make my father direct his anger toward me and eventually I would tell him where the works were.

But like all drug addicts, my parents eventually reached rock bottom and made the decision to try and do something about it. They both started taking methadone, which was supposed to help you get away from the effects of heroin. It's hard to say what my father was thinking at the time, but my mother was just tired of the addiction and of having to do what she had to do. Using methadone was helping her, but my father's habit was just too powerful for him to do what he had to do to keep their relationship together. The methadone treatment just wasn't working for him.

That he continued to get high was very obvious the few times we tried to have a father-and-son moment. We used to go to the movies a lot, and he would usually be high as hell. I would be watching a movie and I would turn to my dad and he would be nodding out. He did that several times, and we would always end up leaving the theater.

My mother was still seeing men at the time, and she ended up meeting this guy named Michael Johnson. He was a cool guy who had just come out of a marriage. They ended up falling in love, and Michael asked my mother to marry him.

We were still in Santa Ana and I was still running with F Troop. But one day something happened that changed all that.

I was hanging out with a few of my friends. We were all leaning against this van and all of a sudden this car pulled up. Someone in the car wanted to know where we were from, which in those days meant he wanted to know our gang affiliation. I don't remember who said it, but somebody yelled, "F Troop!" The next thing I knew, I heard this bang and the guy standing a couple of feet away from me just dropped. I thought, *Holy shit!*

All of a sudden there were bullets flying everywhere.

Everybody scattered. I jumped over a brick wall. You could hear the bullets hitting the wall, the sound of metal hitting stone. I took off running and headed straight home. The guy standing next to me was killed. A few inches the other way and it could have been me. I was lucky. Almost dying had a big impact on me at that moment. I knew this was not the life I wanted.

Word of the shooting got back to my mother and she said, "That's it, we're getting out of Santa Ana. Pack your bags; we're leaving." I couldn't argue with her. Santa Ana was a rough place, and there were rival gangs everywhere.

My parents had separated by this time. My father had gone to live in my grandmother's house. To be honest, I don't remember much about the day they broke up. I was excited that my mother had given up going with the men and the drugs and that I was getting a second chance to be around a lifestyle that was different than what I was used to. Looking back on it, all I can say is that my mother getting up and leaving my father like that was a very strong, brave thing to do.

I wasn't going to have to worry about my parents doing drugs anymore and I could stop making excuses and start bringing my friends around to my house. It seemed like for the first time in my life, I would have a chance at a normal life. But there was one more thing I had to deal with before we left Santa Ana.

I had to get jumped out of F Troop.

It wasn't like it is now in gangs where you can be killed if you try to get out. All I had to do was get the shit beat out of me again. So I went to the gang and told them I was leaving town and it was like I thought. They said, "You got jumped in, you've gotta get jumped out." So I went through the whole thing. I got beat on again. But this time, when the first guy who punched me, I punched back. At one point I had four guys on top of me at once and I was getting stomped into the floor. But I was fighting back the whole time. Finally it was over and I was all bloody again. But I hurt a few guys too. The guys in F Troop wished me good luck and told me to have a good life.

And just like that I was out of the gang life.

We moved back to Huntington Beach when I was thirteen and ended up renting Walter Blanchard's house. A lot had changed with my brothers since we had last been together. Jim had a girlfriend and had moved in with her. Marty moved back in with us. Mike was in juvenile hall for assault. Mike was the first one in our family to use cocaine, and that put him over the edge. Drugs really fucked up his brain.

I was staying away from gangs and that kind of thing, but not long after we moved back to Huntington Beach, I still found myself in situations where I would have to fight.

I entered junior high school at Dwyer Middle School. Even though I was no longer in a gang, I thought that I was still a bit of a gangbanger and I dressed the part. There was this Mexican kid named Mario Muñoz, and for some reason he had a problem with the way I was dressed. One day we stood off in the hallway and he said, "Let's fight."

Well, everybody gathered around and started yelling, "Fight! Fight!" I told him to meet me in the park after school so we wouldn't get in trouble. That afternoon, the final bell rang and we all ran to the park. I had a Mercedes-Benz hood ornament that I had ripped off a car and was holding it in my hand. Mario had nothing. I swung at him and missed. Suddenly somebody in the crowd threw a chain to Mario.

Wow! This is not fair at all, I thought.

Then somebody threw me a skateboard.

Now I had a weapon. All of a sudden it was fair.

Mario swung at me with the chain and I blocked it. Then he swung again and hit me in the back. I dropped the skateboard and I started crying. I tried to swing at him again, but he swung first and hit me on the top of my arm.

All of a sudden my brother came running across the park.

Our house was right across the street, and he was looking out the window when he saw what was going on. He ran up to us, tried to stop the fight, and ended up getting right in the middle of it and chasing Mario away.

Huntington Beach. Santa Ana. It was just one fight after another wherever I went. But at least now I was home.

CHAPTER FIVE

High School, My School

I guess you could say I was still pretty much a juvenile delinquent after we moved back to Huntington Beach.

My life was a little bit more stable without all the drug shit going on in the house, and although I was still hanging around with some tough characters, I was not in a gang anymore. But I was reaching out for attention more than I had before because I still wasn't getting it at home.

Almost immediately, I began causing trouble at Dwyer Middle School. I hated to wake up in the morning and I would be late a lot. I know I set a record at Dwyer for having the most detentions in a single year in the history of the school. I think the tally was something like sixty-four. While I was at Dwyer I was sent to the school psychologist a couple of times and my parents were brought in. Everybody knew I was troublesome. I was a lousy student and a bad kid so they just pushed me into the eighth grade. All they wanted was to get me out of the school as soon as possible.

I was still doing drugs. And my mother knew it. I remember she would find out that I was sniffing glue and she would tell me not to. I would tell her "Okay" and then go off and sniff glue again. Nobody could tell me what to do at that point. And I never did drugs alone. Because as far back as I can remember there was always somebody around who was doing them too.

I remember when I was in the sixth grade, there was this guy who lived in an apartment across the street from us. He had this old beat-up Cadillac sitting out front that was spray painted with the initials LAPD. I wasn't sure at the time, but I thought he might have been a musician or somebody heavily into music. We used to hang out and smoke pot.

I had a friend named Nathan in the seventh grade, and we were both into cocaine at the time. We'd steal stereos and shit and sell them on the black market to pay for our habit. We'd go buy the cocaine, hook it up, and smoke it. For little kids, we knew a lot about drugs. We knew how to make rock and smoke it. During that time I also took acid, mushrooms, and PCP. A lot of that stuff was just a onetime thing. I would try just about anything at least once. Except heroin. I knew enough to never go near that. But besides heroin, I was into a lot of crazy shit for a young kid.

Like the time my friend and I attempted a strong-arm robbery of a complete stranger. One night I was drinking with some friends and we decided we were going to rob somebody. So we went down to this bar called Taxi's. After a while this guy came out of the bar and we jumped him. He managed to get away and run back into the bar. A minute later he came running out after us with a bunch of his buddies and we took off.

They were chasing us down the street. It was then that I decided to let them catch up with me, so I slowed down and joined the group that had been chasing us. I was yelling stuff like, "Let's get those guys!" and they thought I was one of them. They kept running, and I broke off from them and went home.

Easily the highlight of my junior high school crime spree was when I snuck into the post office and stole the American flag that was hanging there. I ended up keeping that flag for years, until one day I was looking for it and it had just disappeared. Ironically, I think somebody stole it from me.

I started my first year of high school at Huntington Beach High School. My freshman year was more about learning who I was at school than actually learning anything academic. I wasn't sure if I was in the right classes or who I should be hanging out with. I looked a lot like a white kid, but I was still hanging out with the Mexican kids.

There was Ricky and Nacho—guys I had known from my elementary school days. After school, we would always go out and cause some kind of trouble. We'd run around town spray painting walls, do drugs, go fishing, and, of course, steal things like fishing poles and all kinds of other stuff.

We never had problems with the law. We did everything so clean that we never got stopped or caught. I have no idea how I got so good at stealing. Practice, I suppose. But some-times I think it was God looking over me, saying that he was going to let me get away with this stuff for now.

I was still a virgin during my first year in high school. Not that I wasn't interested in sex. When I was growing up I used to watch porn with my brothers, and I was very curious when it came to sex. I had heard stories from guys, and I was real anxious to find out what it was all about.

Then shortly after my sixteenth birthday, I got involved with this girl named Danielle. She was an older woman—a junior and a cheerleader. One thing led to another, and I finally had sex for the first time. It was my first real relation-ship with a woman. Danielle and I were on and off for about eight months, and then we broke up.

I continued to see my father once in a while for holidays or just to hang out. I still loved him no matter what. But he was still on drugs and I didn't trust him. And with good reason.

Before my parents split up, when I was way into fishing, I remember getting two brand-new fishing poles. Not long after getting them, I put them out behind the house before I went to bed. I woke up the next morning, and the fishing poles were gone. Later I found out that my dad had sold them to get money for drugs. That hurt. When I turned sixteen, I got a moped from a friend and my dad asked me if he could borrow it. When he hadn't returned it after a few days I went to see him and he told me he sold it to get drug money. I was really disappointed in him.

As messed up as my dad was, toward the end of my freshman year I can honestly say I was well on the road to being a serious juvenile delinquent.

JOYCE ROBLES *I remember coming home one day during Tito's sophomore year in high school and finding Tito, Nacho, and Ricky doing drugs in our backyard. I chased the boys away and then took Tito in the house. I just snapped. I told Tito that those boys were going down a wrong path and they wanted to take him with them. There were tears rolling down his face. The next day he brought over Eric Escobedo, who was a good kid. Nacho and Ricky kept coming around for a while, but I told them not to stop by anymore.*

I started hanging out more and more with my friend Eric Escobedo, who was on the high school wrestling team. We wrestled a bit and I remember him throwing me around like a rag doll. But it seemed kind of cool, so I thought I'd try this wrestling thing out.

When I walked into the wrestling room to sign up, the first thing I asked was, "Where's the ring?" The coach was a guy named Bob Rice and he told me that there was no ring in wrestling and that I was thinking about professional wrestling, which, he said, was totally fake.

"It's not fake," I told him.

But whether it was fake or not, I suddenly felt that, in wrestling, I might have found something that worked for me. It was a one-on-one sport, and the only person who could make me better was myself. I didn't have to depend on anybody else.

I was a pretty small kid, so the coach had me wrestle a couple of the varsity guys just to see what I could do. They were throwing me around pretty good, but at one point, I caught a guy in a headlock and started to pull back on his head in imitation of what I had seen the pros do. The coach stepped in and said, "No, you can't do that. You've got to put his arm in there." That was my official introduction to high school wrestling. The coach showed me the move and I began to hit some of the varsity guys with it. I thought, *Wow! This is cool!*

But I had a lot to learn.

The first person I actually wrestled in a real match was this kid named Michael Biss from Westchester High School. The match started, he shot in, took me down, cradled me, put me on my back, and pinned me in the first period. I got up and was so mad that I started crying and yelling. Then I asked Coach Rice what had gone wrong. "Well, he took you down, put you in a cradle, and pinned you," he said.

"What's a cradle?" I asked.

Coach said, "I'll show you tomorrow at practice."

My attitude at that moment was that I wanted to know what had happened, why it happened, and what I could do to fix it and make it better. Coach showed me the move and how to get out of it. Eric and I would practice during class and stay after class to practice some more. Drill after drill, repetition after repetition. On the weekends we'd go back to Eric's house and we'd drill some more.

I won my second match. Pinned the guy with a head and arm hold. I was immediately put on the varsity team in my freshman year and I lettered on my very first try. I was a pretty happy guy.

My stepfather, Mike, was big into sports and NASCAR racing, and he was always telling me stories. He was a pretty good guy, but I was pretty rebellious against him because he wasn't my father. I stole his car a couple of times. He never hit me, but I would get grounded a lot. He did as good a job as he could at the time.

JOYCE ROBLES *My husband, Mike, and Tito were getting along pretty well. Mike was a strict, hard-labor kind of guy, but I remember the really nice things. Like the time he sewed Tito's first wrestling letter on his jacket. Tito would occasionally make some money on the fishing boats, and Mike would automatically double whatever he made.*

Things changed once I got into wrestling. Now all of a sudden I was forced to get good grades; if I didn't, I wouldn't be able to wrestle. So when I started my sophomore year I was doing my homework, trying to get to school on time, and putting in an effort to learn. I couldn't just get by anymore. I had to get good grades or I couldn't compete.

As soon as wrestling season was over, I was back doing the same old shit, going out and partying with friends, stealing shit, and doing drugs. But during wrestling season I was home all the time. Some of my friends started asking if I was going to become a professional wrestler. All I would do was laugh at them and say, "You never know what's going to happen."

By the time the freshman-sophomore season started I was wrestling on the varsity squad in the 152-pound weight group. That year I ended up with a 25–15 record. I was one of the top wrestlers on the team. One of my more satisfying victories came when I stomped this kid Jerry Bohlander. Remember that name. Jerry ended up figuring in my future plans.

Because I was on the wrestling team, people started to notice me. All of a sudden I wasn't just the big guy who was always getting into trouble. Now I was hot shit.

But I was far from a ladies' man in high school. I was a shy kid when it came to girls. There were girls who I liked, but I was just too shy to say anything to them. I did have a girlfriend in high school named Heather. We dated for about two and a half years, and then she broke up with me to date somebody else.

I met Kristin during my sophomore year. Her family was originally from Arizona, then they moved to Nebraska for a while, and then to Huntington Beach. I remember walking to my classroom one day as Kristin walked by. I turned around and said, "Shit! That chick's hot."

I had no idea that she even knew I existed. For better or worse I had developed a reputation around school as being a tough guy. So my guess at the time was that she probably would not have been interested in me because she thought I was some kind of hood.

I told my friend Eric Escobedo, "There's this chick; I don't know her name. She has sandy blonde hair and she's hot!" Five days later Kristin and Eric were going out.

I told Eric he was a fucking asshole.

CHAPTER SIX

Hard Knocks, Hard Time

I finished my sophomore year with a 3.46 grade point average. Want to know what I did on my summer vacation? I stole a car.

And went to jail.

This is the way it went down. My friends and I used to go up and down streets and if the cars were open, we'd get in there and take the change, stereos, speakers—anything in the car we could get something out of or sell. This one time I had been drinking with some friends and we hit this car. I pulled the visor down and the keys dropped right into my lap. I decided to take it for a cruise.

I started the car and drove it around for a while. It was a stick shift and I didn't know how to drive stick shift, so I was grinding the shit out of it but driving well enough to get around. After a while I pulled into Eric's driveway, but I couldn't stop and ended up slamming into one of his aunt's cars. Instead of calling my parents, Eric's family called the cops. The cops came and arrested me for grand theft auto.

I went to court, was found guilty, and was sentenced to juvenile hall for a total of thirty-nine days.

The biggest thing I had to get used to in being institutionalized was having to live by a strict schedule. You were up at six in the morning. You had your breakfast pushed through a slot in your cell door. Then you'd go to school for four hours, come back to your cell for lunch, and then go back to school for another hour and a half. Then it was dinner, shower after dinner, and, for me, a lot of push-ups and triceps workouts.

I avoided having problems with other inmates by just keeping my nose out of other people's business. But there was this one kid who tried to give me a hard time. I just turned around, punched him in the stomach, and knocked the wind out of him. I turned and walked away. No one ever bothered me after that.

Once summer vacation was over, I was back at school. And once the wrestling season started, I was the same good student. When it came to wrestling I was suddenly real goal-oriented. I wanted to get the most pins. I wanted to be a CIF (California Interscholastic Federation) champion. I wanted to be a state champion. By that time I had grown to six foot one and weighed around one hundred eighty-five pounds.

Paul Herrera took over as wrestling coach my junior year. He was like a big brother to me. He was like the dad I never had. He'd wake me up for school in the morning. He made sure I kept my grades up and stayed eligible. That year we were first in league and second in CIF.

But once wrestling season was over, I went back to being a hood.

My friends and I would stake out houses. We'd see when people would go off to work and when they would come back. We'd watch a house for three or four days, then watch for another week, and then that third week we would wait for them to go to work, bust out a side window, unlock the house, back a car in, fill the car up with stuff, and take off. We did that for a good four months. It was going along fine for a while, and then we nearly got caught a couple of times and we finally decided to stop doing it.

I turned seventeen that year. I loved wrestling. But when I wasn't on the mat I always seemed to be looking for trouble. Or, as it sometimes happened, trouble came looking for me.

One day I was standing in the hallway at school with my girlfriend Heather and this guy walked by and said, "Hey, you fucking cunt!" I turned around and said, "What did you say?" He got right up in my face and said, "I called her a fucking cunt. What are you going to do about it?"

I said, "Are you serious? I'm going to beat your fucking ass!"

He was standing there with all his buddies and I was by myself so he was acting real brave. He said, "We'll see." And then he turned around and walked away. The next day I came to school and he was standing by himself in the cafeteria. I came up behind him and shoved him super hard. He turned around and his eyes were all wide.

"Remember you talking your fucking shit?" I yelled at him. "What are you going to do about it now?"

I punched him once, dislocating his collarbone and breaking his shoulder. I looked at him real hard for a second, then turned around and went off to class. Two periods rolled by and I was sitting at my desk when all of a sudden the door opened and John Ortiz, the campus cop, walked in and told me to get up. He said that I was under arrest for assault, handcuffed me, and took me out of the classroom.

I went to trial, was found guilty, and was sentenced to juvenile hall for twenty-three days.

It was pretty much the same situation as the summer before. I was really cool and because of that nobody really messed with me. One day one of the teachers in juvenile hall came up to me and said he had heard I had wrestled in county. I told him I did and that I wished that I had some way to train in here. He asked if I had ever thought about running. It turns out that there was a five-K run coming up and if I wanted, he would make sure that I could do it. There was an incentive, of course. If I did it, I would be able to get sodas and candy (which were a luxury in that place) and I would be able to work out in the weight room. So I went ahead and did the five K and actually ended up taking fifth place. But I couldn't walk for two days afterward because I was so damned sore.

A week before I was set to get out, this kid came up to me

and said, "Listen, homes, you're not going anywhere. We're going to fight, you're going to be extended, and you're going to be here just as long as I am." I told him that wasn't happening.

I hit him right in the gut, he dropped, and I turned around and walked away. He didn't even touch me.

I got out and went back to school. It was time for wrestling and I had to declare an official weight for the CIF. I weighed 174 at the time and the coach wanted me to fight at 160, which meant that I had nine days to cut fourteen pounds before the official weigh-in. Fourteen pounds is not a lot of weight to lose in nine days, but for me cutting that weight was very difficult. So for the next nine days I was spending time in the sauna, doing jumping jacks, and riding the stationary bike. Finally it was the day of the official weigh-ins and I stepped on the scale.

I weighed 160.8. I was less than a pound over the limit.

I started crying and begging the CIF people to give me another chance. I went to the locker room and made myself gag so I could get more water out of me. After about a half hour of doing that, I walked back out and said, "Let's try it again." My weight was 160 on the dot. The athletic commission passed me and let me go. That season we went to the CIF and took third.

By my senior year I had been put in remedial classes. A lot of it had to do with problems I was having at home. I was still doing a lot of shit, staying out late and doing drugs with my friends Nacho and Ricky, who were in a gang on the south side of Huntington Beach. But I wasn't into bang-ing and all that crazy stuff by that time. If anything like that came up, I would just steer away.

I got into trouble when I wasn't wrestling, but during the season I was really solid and gung ho. And being that way might just have saved my life. Nacho called me one day and said that his gang was going to do a couple of drop-offs. They were getting paid money for it, and he said that I should come out with them. I said, "Man, I've got wrestling practice tomorrow. I can't do it."

Nacho kept at me, saying, "You'll be cool and we'll be back real quick." I kept saying I couldn't do it and finally he said, "All right, whatever," and hung up. I went to wrestling practice the next day and didn't think anything of it. When I came home, the phone rang and it was Nacho's mom.

Nacho had gotten arrested. At the time he was in posses-sion of a million dollars' worth of speed, five assault rifles, and five bulletproof vests that he was taking from one gang to another.

Nacho ended up getting twenty-five years to life. He's still in prison to this day. I could have been right there with him.

I'd like to think I have a kind of intuition about these things, that I know enough not to get involved in situations that don't sound right. But that thing with Nacho? I mean, who knows? Not being in the middle of that could have just as easily been plain luck.

I had a great senior year. I was CIF champion, I was

number one in the league and number one in the county. My record was 56–3, with 36 pins. I got my name on the wall of the wrestling room. I was doing well.

And not too long after I turned eighteen, I graduated from high school. But even that didn't go off without a hitch.

June 14, 1993. I had my cap and gown and was all ready to go to the graduation ceremony when I was told that I couldn't cross the stage to accept my diploma in jeans and tennis shoes. I said, "What do you mean? I've done so much." They said sorry.

So I ran home and got my brother's khaki pants that were too big for me, put on some black shoes, and ran back to the school just in time to graduate with the rest of my class. It had been a long, hard struggle, but I had finally made it. I graduated. My next question was, "Okay, what do I do now?" I didn't have any money from my parents to go to college. I really didn't have any expectations of what I wanted to do with my life. I was just happy that I graduated from high school.

I went through the summer not doing much of anything. Just hanging out. Partying. Doing drugs. As usual, I really did not have a clue what to do next. I sensed that I might be going down the wrong road and that I could very easily end up in prison or dead and that nobody would even remember me at all.

I was still living at home, but things were getting tense in the house.

JOYCE ROBLES *For a long time, Mike had problems with Tito's brother Marty. Marty was still living at home and would rather surf than work, so he and Mike were always getting into it. Tito saw what was going on between them and he hated Mike for it.*

I thought everything was okay between Mike and me. But then my mother came up to me one day, handed me $800, and said, "Your stepfather wants you to leave."

And just like that, I was out.

CHAPTER SEVEN

Love and Odd Jobs

My stepfather's position was that I was eighteen, I had caused too much fucking trouble in the house, and it was time for me to be a man and stand on my own two feet. And you know what? His attitude didn't really surprise me. I wasn't doing much around the house except getting high and getting into trouble.

I had to agree with him that it was time for me to go.

JOYCE ROBLES *I was crying the day Tito packed his things. I told him he could stay as long as he was in school. He said, "I don't want to be in this man's house." I think in Tito's mind, he felt alienated from me as well. For a long time after that I felt that Tito hated me.*

So I moved in with my brother Marty and his girlfriend. I agreed to pay him $200 a month in rent and I used the

$800 my mother gave me to buy a car. So I had a place to stay and a car to drive around. All I could think at that point was, "Now what?"

For a while I continued to think about college. Paul Herrera had gone off to Ocean View to teach, and I had thought about hooking up with him again. But I didn't have the money to go out there and I couldn't get a wrestling scholarship because they were looking at guys who had done a lot better than me. And I knew I didn't have the grades to get into a decent college.

So I decided to just take whatever job I could get. I did a little bit of construction, but I didn't like it that much. Then I got a job with Allied Moving Services, which was hard work. I was working sixteen- to eighteen-hour days on an almost daily basis. It was at that point that I started doing methamphetamine in order to stay up and be able to work longer days.

It was also around that time that I began dealing drugs.

I had never really thought about dealing drugs before. Using drugs? Sure, every chance I had. Dealing was a different story. It was like stepping over a line that I wasn't sure I wanted to cross.

But one day somebody turned me on to some pot and I asked him if he could turn me on to some more because I knew a lot of people who were always looking to score. Then people started asking for meth and that's when I started dealing meth.

My conscience would bother me sometimes. There were

times when I thought I was going down the same road as my parents. But the more I thought about it, the more I realized that I really didn't care. I was making money and taking care of business. And I was always very careful and very sharp when I was dealing. Never came close to getting caught. That went on for about a year. I was working, dealing, and once in a while I would steal food or things that I could sell.

For a while I worked as a bouncer at a club called Mazzotti's. Mazzotti's was a pretty easy gig for the most part, just checking IDs and monitoring the line and letting people go in and out. Normally, things at the club were pretty cool, but there were those times when stuff just happened.

One night this guy came to the front of the line. You could tell he really didn't know anybody, but he acted like he did. And he just walked right past me. I stopped him and said, "Hold on, man! There's a line here."

He said, "I don't wait in any lines."

My response was, "I don't know you. You wait in line."

He said, "Whatever," and then tried to walk past me.

I smacked him down and got him in a front headlock, picked him up off his feet, walked him out the door, and threw him into the street. This guy deserved to be made an example of and, at age nineteen, I was very much into making an example of people and putting them in their place.

Meanwhile, wrestling had gone out the window. I wasn't training anymore—there didn't seem to be any reason to.

It was around that time that I reconnected with Kristin.

We ran into each other at a house party one night and started talking. Not too long after that we started hanging out regularly. But just as friends. It went on like that for about a year. Then in 1995 we went to the movies to see *Interview with a Vampire.* Right in the middle of the movie I started getting real nervous. I was thinking, *Holy shit! We're on a date right now.* We went back to her apartment afterward and fooled around, but we didn't have sex. We both knew that we were falling in love. We were with each other every single day after that.

Everything about being with Kristin just felt right. She came from a really good family. Her parents were straitlaced. Her father was a CEO at a hospital and her mother was Mary Poppins. I felt that Kristin might have been acting out a lot because of her family background.

Although we were always together, we would not live together until 1996. Her parents were paying for her apartment. I still had to worry about coming up with rent money. I was still working at Allied Moving Services and dealing and she was working at a sandwich shop. We were both partying a lot. I still had no direction and no clue about what I wanted to do with the rest of my life. But I was in a serious relationship for the first time in my life with somebody I loved. That felt good.

And everywhere we turned in our Huntington Beach neighborhood, there seemed to be music. Hard-core music.

I had always been into punk and the really heavy hard-core and metal. When I was in high school I would always have songs by the likes of White Zombie and Pantera blasting in the background when I was practicing my wrestling moves.

There was this band that used to practice near Huntington Beach that everybody said was fucking good called KoRn. One day Kristin and I grabbed our fake IDs and went to the Club 5902 to hear them play. We were standing in line when all of a sudden Reggie, a guy from my block, walked by. I yelled out his name and he turned around. We started talking and we told him that we were there to see KoRn. Reggie said, "KoRn is my band. I'm the bass player." He got us right in.

The band started playing and a mosh pit immediately formed. I was right in the middle of it, knocking people down. I got real tight with the band after that and we would show up at their gigs at places like the Whisky or Fullerton College. The guys in KoRn were all party guys and we would always party together. Then they got real big and next thing you know they were driving around in BMWs and Mercedes. I was real impressed by their success. It was my first contact with people who had gone from nothing to being millionaires with lots of money and big cars. I wanted to know how I could get all that.

Kristin and I continued to make ends meet. I had this feeling that somehow I wanted the spotlight. And I knew that it wasn't going to happen by moving furniture and dealing drugs.

KRISTIN ORTIZ *At first I didn't know that Tito was doing drugs and involved in illegal activities. I came from a good family, and I guess I was kind of naïve. I always liked the bad boy. Maybe I just tried to avoid knowing. But I learned about six months into our relationship when Tito borrowed my car to go get me a birthday present. When he came back to the house he had this huge bubble-gum machine with him. I realized then that he might have stolen it. The next day my mom got a phone call from the Huntington Beach police department. A notebook of mine had fallen out of the car at the restaurant where he had stolen the bubble-gum machine. My mom was so angry that she grabbed Tito by the ear, made him return the bubble-gum machine, and then made him turn himself in to the police. He was charged with a felony and spent two weeks in jail.*

Later that year I was in a bar when I ran into Paul Herrera. We started talking and catching up on old times. He wanted to know what I was doing and asked me if I ever thought about wrestling again.

I told him I would love to but I would have no way of paying for it. He said, "I'll tell you what. I can guarantee you we can get you some financial aid. You've been on your own for the past two years and supporting yourself. And being Mexican, that should help you out a bit. I'll call Raoul

Duarte, who is the wrestling coach over at Golden West College, and we'll see what we can do. Why don't you come down to the college tomorrow and meet with him."

I told Paul that I was working the next day and couldn't make it.

Paul just looked at me for a second and then said, "Well, take your choice. What do you want to do?" I went home that night and went to bed, but I couldn't sleep. I stayed up all night thinking about what Paul had said. I got up the next morning, looked in the bathroom mirror, and I didn't recognize myself.

I was six foot two, one hundred eighty pounds, and I was out of shape. I had black circles under my eyes, pimples all over my face. I looked like a drug addict. It was all the meth and the alcohol. I really didn't know the person who was staring back at me. At that moment I had a reality check.

I called my boss Monday morning and I told him that I couldn't come in that day.

"What do you mean you can't come in today?" he yelled. "We need you here. We don't have an ass to fill your spot." I told him that I had to talk to some people at school, that I might have an opportunity for a scholarship. My boss said, "You don't come in today, don't worry about coming in again, you'll be fired."

"In that case I quit," I said, and hung up the phone.

So I went down to the school and walked into Raoul Duarte's office. We talked for a while and I told him I wanted to see what we could do about getting me into school. We went down to the financial aid office and pretty soon I had financial aid that was paying for my tuition, my books, and part of my rent. All of a sudden I had another chance to come back and wrestle.

I started at Golden West College in the fall of 1995. I moved to a place that was closer to school. My major was physical education and my minor was special education. At that point I wanted to be a teacher. I thought it would be cool to be able to give something back to kids.

When I first got to school, I knew I wanted to stick with it and make it work. Kristin was totally in my corner. She enrolled as well, and we ended up taking some classes together. She would pat me on the back and support me. And it was working. I was doing my homework. I was showing up for school every day. Once in a while I would be late, but most of the time, I was on time.

I like to think that I was using the opportunity to learn some things rather than just use college as an excuse to wrestle. Looking back, it was like I was taking classes that I sensed would help me at some point in the future. The big thing for me was the speech classes I took. Those classes taught me how to be comfortable speaking in front of large groups. I learned that if I could engage people in a way that made sense to them, then they would listen and then, hopefully, the next time they would understand.

KRISTIN ORTIZ *That first year in Golden West was great. We went to school together, we even took a couple of classes*

together. I would help him with his homework.
For the first time in his life, Tito was focused on
school.

I was real excited the first day I showed up for wrestling
practice. So was the coach. Until he saw the monitoring
band around my ankle. At first the other wrestlers thought it
was some kind of jewelry. It was really the result of my latest
brush with the law.

Shortly before I started at Golden West College, I was
arrested for burglary. A friend and I had gotten drunk one
night and decided to go hit some cars for stereos. This time
we got caught. I was given five days in the Orange County
Jail, which I served without any problems, and then was
given thirty days of house arrest. I couldn't go more than a
hundred yards from my house unless it was to go to school
or wrestling. Kristin was pissed. She really busted my chops
on that one. She kind of understood, given my upbringing,
but boy, was she mad at me for jeopardizing my chance at
having a future.

The coach had no complaints once he saw me wrestle. I
would cover the ankle monitor with a protective pad during
practice. I actually shorted the monitor out one time because
of all the sweat getting into it and it had to be replaced.

Once I started wrestling, I began to do things that pointed
to the beginning of the larger-than-life Tito Ortiz. I started
dying my hair a different color before each tournament. I

did that just because I wanted to, but I found out that people who didn't normally go to wrestling tournaments started showing up for no other reason than to see what color my hair was that week.

I was awesome that first year. I did well in the state and regional meets and had the most pins. I went undefeated and I won the state title. It was hard work, but I really dedicated myself.

To the point where I almost killed myself.

At one point during the season, I had to drop down from my walking-around weight of 205. So I started running. I ran for days trying to get that weight off. One day I was out running and I told myself, "I can't run anymore." I collapsed in front of a Taco Bell and just lay there. I called Kristin to come and pick me up. She pulled up and just stared at me laying on the ground.

"Are you okay?" she asked.

I was fine, but losing that weight was such a hard cut that I decided that whatever my walking-around weight was, it was going to be the weight I would wrestle at from now on.

Although I put a lot of my energy into the sport, the reality was that I had no real interest in pursuing it professionally at that point. My plan was to get my degree in physical education and work as a wrestling coach and as a special education teacher. During my first year at Golden West, I received a phone call from a friend of mine who was a wrestling coach at Marina High School. He wanted to know if I was interested in being his assistant. Since my career was going in that direction, it seemed like a way to get my foot in the door.

I was passionate about working with those kids and making them better both as wrestlers and as people. I was only a bit older, so they could relate to me. I was their confidant; if they had problems with girlfriends or things at home, they would come to me. It was funny, the first person to ever give me a bloody nose in a wrestling ring was one of those Marina High kids.

Around that time I got hooked on this television program called *Ultimate Fighting Championship*. It was like a combination of boxing, martial arts, and street fighting. I was amazed at what I was seeing. The stuff was crazy, and the guys who were doing it had to be nuts. Ultimate fighting, or, as it's sometimes called, mixed martial arts, was in its infancy at that point. Not a lot of people knew about it compared to mainstream boxing or professional wrestling, and a lot of people put it down as being a barbaric blood sport. All I knew was that I was fascinated.

I became even more interested the day I was watching a UFC fight on television when all of a sudden I thought, *Damn, that guy looks familiar.* It was Jerry Bohlander. All I could think of was, *I manhandled that guy in high school and now he's doing this stuff?*

Not long after wrestling season, Paul Herrera got ahold of me and said there was this Ultimate Fighting guy named

Tank Abbott who was looking for somebody to train with and would I be interested? Paul suggested that since I was doing so well in college, I might be interested in giving mixed martial arts a try.

I hadn't really given much thought to the idea. I was doing well in the amateur wrestling ranks. But I wasn't planning on turning pro—nor was I being asked to—so I figured as long as this guy Tank didn't hurt me, I guess I could train with him. So I went and worked with him for a few weeks.

At the time I thought Tank was a pretty cool guy. I was his wrestling partner and that was it. I didn't put on the gloves and spar with him. We just did jujitsu and wrestling, so I didn't have to worry about throwing punches and kicks. He really didn't take too well to the wrestling part of mixed martial arts. I was taking him down at will and he was getting frustrated. Wrestling was his weakness, and he took what I was trying to teach him grudgingly.

But he taught me a lot about molding the persona of a fighter. He taught me that if you talk the smack, when it comes down to fight time, it doesn't matter if you win or lose. You talk the smack to make people either love you or hate you. Once they love you or hate you, then they'll talk about you. If they stop talking about you, then you've got problems.

I had a good time with Tank and worked with him through the summer. Then I went back to school in the fall of 1996. I had another good season, and I went on to win the state title again.

Then in March of 1997, I got a call from Tank Abbott.

He wanted to know if I wanted to fight on an Ultimate Fighting Championship card. At first I wasn't sure. I knew how to wrestle and to street fight a little bit. But I had never done anything with punches and elbows before.

The owner of UFC at the time was a guy named Bob Meyerwitz. The events were typically selling out ten-thousand-seat arenas, and the pay-per-view shows were typically getting a half-million buys, which was not too shabby.

The organization seemed to be coming into its own slowly but surely. But then Bob got a little arrogant and told Ted Turner that he was going to be the biggest thing in sports and that he didn't care if Turner carried the show on cable or not. Turner's response was, "Okay, we're going to stop you." And since UFC basically didn't have any rules at the time, it became an easy target. Senator John McCain started speaking out against it and pretty soon UFC was off the bigger cable channels and regulated to basic channels. But even though I knew enough about the history of the organization to know that it was on a downhill slide by that time, I was still interested in getting involved.

They approached me to fight as an amateur, which was the only way I would even consider fighting. I was on a scholarship for wrestling. I would've lost that if I had fought for money. So as long as I could fight as an amateur, I thought I'd give it a shot.

I started training with Tank Abbott late in 1997. Training for my first fight took six months. We would practice wrestling and jujitsu, we'd do a little bit of sparring like boxers do, and we'd run and lift weights. It was hard work, but I picked up on it really quickly.

In a sense I had become Tank Jr. But as we continued to train, I found that there were some definite differences between us. I brought the hard training and the work ethic to the relationship. I worked my butt off, but Tank was always looking for the easy way out. He partied all the time. Tank's attitude was always: "I'm going to fight and kick people's asses, then go out and get drunk, and then go fight some more." He was a fighter; he was no martial artist. His style was that of a bar brawler.

A lot of people who have followed my career think that it began with the UFC. But they're wrong. I just haven't talked about the very first fight I had until now. It wasn't really a legal, sanctioned fight, and it does not count on my professional record, but here it is . . .

A few weeks before my UFC debut, I accepted an offer by a promoter named Larry Landis to fight this jujitsu guy in a high school gym in Rosemead, California. I took the fight as kind of checkpoint: I figured if I was going to fight in the UFC, I'd better see what I had at that point. The fight went to a draw—the main reason being that I was not real good at submissions back then and these jujitsu guys could take a pounding really well. But I can tell you that I gave this guy one of the worst beatings that he'd ever had in his life. And after that fight, I knew I was ready.

The first time I fought in an Ultimate Fighting Championship event was on May 30, 1997. The event was called

UFC 13: The Ultimate Force and I was fighting for Team Tank. When I entered the arena that night, I didn't really know what to expect. There were about ten thousand screaming people in the stands, and the atmosphere of the place was just crazy. At that point, people saw UFC fights as human cockfights with no rules and no time limits. But there were rules, and each fight consisted of one fifteen-minute round.

I remember climbing into the ring and pacing back and forth in the corner of the Octagon. I was thinking, *Holy shit! I'm here! Don't make a mistake.*

The guy I was fighting that night was Wes Albritton. Wes had a fifth-degree black belt in karate but no wrestling experience. The way the fight was promoted, Wes was on the striking side of the sport and I was on the grappling side of it.

The fight lasted twenty-two seconds. I remember the bell ringing and I immediately got into a clinch. I grabbed a double underhook on him, body locked him, and threw him to the ground. Then I sat on his chest and started laying in punches. I won with a technical knockout for strikes.

I was pumped. For me, it was a competition; I was competing to see who was the better man. That's how I felt about it. The experience was really cool. Since it was on television, all my friends got to see me beating somebody up and I wasn't getting in trouble for doing it. I was real pumped when we went back to the dressing room. And then I found out that I was going to have to fight again!

It turns out that one of the four guys who was supposed

to move on to the next round had gotten injured. I had been named his alternate, so before I could catch my breath, they put me back in and I was fighting in the finals.

When I got back into the ring later that night, I was facing this guy named Guy Mezger. I remember walking back out and thinking, *Oh shit! Who is this guy?* Mezger was a pro. He had been fighting out of Japan for a time and he had championship credentials. I was still pumped from my first match, and my feeling going into this fight was that I was going to hit him real hard and get this thing over with.

The fight started and I was dominating him. I had him in the position to cradle and I was kneeing him in the head. Suddenly the referee stepped in and stopped it. Mezger was bleeding, but at that time, the UFC never stopped a fight for bleeding. Unfortunately, the perception of Team Tank was that we were all thug guys who talked shit and started trouble. And because I was on Team Tank, the referee automatically didn't like me much.

So he stopped the match, checked the cut, and then restarted the match. Mezger threw a punch and hit me. I stepped back and took a shot at him, but when I did that I left my neck exposed. He got a choke on me, pulled on it, and fell on his back.

I tried to pull out, but I didn't know how. I was just too inexperienced—I didn't really know how to train in a professional way. I was new to the fighting techniques and just about everything connected to the sport.

All of a sudden I couldn't breathe anymore. I tapped. The match was over. I lost.

I was so pissed off I got up and started yelling. I was so mad. I thought the way the referee handled the match was bullshit. To this day people come up to me and say that they shouldn't have stopped the match and that I should have won. They may have been right. But at that point, what did I know?

Yeah, I was disappointed. I never liked to lose at anything. But now I had a taste for the UFC. Everything about this kind of fighting excited me. I was still bummed after the fight with Mezger. But back in the dressing room Paul Herrera came up to me all excited.

"You did an awesome job," he told me. "You showed an awesome fight! People loved that fight! Don't be bummed about anything!"

That cheered me up a little bit. But to my way of thinking, a loss was still a loss.

After the fight I went home to Kristin and we decided to go out. We went to a club called the Rhino Room down in Huntington Beach and, as always, we were waiting in line for the door guy to let us come in. All of a sudden, this big security guy comes up to me and says "You're Tito Ortiz! Come on, man! You don't have to wait in line."

When he said that, I was kind of surprised. I had never had a problem waiting in line to get into a place. But being called out like that in front of a lot of people was something new to me.

So we went in and I was thinking that it was pretty cool to be recognized. We went to the bar and I'm about to order drinks when all of a sudden I hear a loud "Hey, Tito!" from the other end of the bar. Everybody in the place turned to look at me. Then this guy comes up to me and says, "Don't worry about it; this drink's on me." I thought, *This is rad—people recognizing me and buying me drinks. This is the attention I've always been looking for. This is cool! Right on!*

All of a sudden I was fighting and people were loving me for it.

CHAPTER EIGHT

Bad Boy, Whatcha Gonna Do?

KRISTIN ORTIZ *Tito had just fought for the first time, and right away I began to notice a change in his personality. He got a little bit of fame and a little bit of money, and the friendship as well as the relationship started to suffer a little bit.*

I finished my second year at Golden State College with a perfect 28–0 record. We won the state title again. But it was just like it had been in high school: I was partying and drinking and doing drugs.

Mostly pot, which I was still dealing to make money. I was still doing meth but not as much as before—sometimes every other week, sometimes once a month. Kristin and I were very into school, and you couldn't do meth and go to school. When I got into Golden West, meth was something I knew I would have to stop, so I actually quit and had withdrawal symptoms. But it was never anything really heavy. All I would do was sleep it off for a couple of days and I would be fine.

When I finished my second year at Golden West in 1996, I was looking to transfer to a four-year school for my junior year. The University of Bakersfield was looking at me. Arizona State was looking at me. Nebraska was looking at me. Nebraska was too cold. Arizona was too hot. And Bakersfield was only a couple of hours away. It was out in the middle of the desert and kind of isolated, but I would be able to wrestle.

Kristin and I discussed my going to Bakersfield. She was working, and so we decided that I would go by myself and that she would join me at the beginning of the second semester.

KRISTIN ORTIZ *I was always paranoid that Tito was probably cheating on me. I began to catch him in lies. He finally did cheat on me and we broke up. We were basically apart for two months. It was horrible. I was devastated. So was Tito. He would write me letters and call my family and friends. He was trying real hard to patch things up with us. So of course, eventually, I forgave him.*

Well, the second semester came around and Kristin still wasn't sure about coming up. Bakersfield was okay. I had some friends up there. I was doing okay in my classes and, of course, there was wrestling. But I was missing Kristin and I was kind of lonely.

That's when I cheated on her for the first time.

The girl was a fitness chick. She trained, so we had something in common. This went on for a while. Then Kristin found out. She was pissed. All I could think of to say was it happened because she was never around. Finally she said, "I'm going to move up there with you or you're going to lose me." I didn't want to lose her, so finally in the third semester, she joined me.

KRISTIN ORTIZ *I went back with him even after I found out he had cheated with somebody at Bakersfield. It was rough and it took a while to heal the relationship, but we got through it.*

That was the first time I cheated, but I was tempted all the time. For a long time I just could not bring myself to do it. I was very persuasive and persistent in trying to convince Kristin that it would never happen again. I knew I had made a mistake.

I was continuing to make a name for myself at Bakersfield, and word of my two UFC fights was getting around. One day this guy named Saul Garcia came to one of our practices. Saul was one of those guys who had been around the business a while and claimed to know people. I know, you hear that all the time. But what did I know?

Anyway, he came up to me after practice and introduced himself. He was real encouraging. He had heard about my fights and said that I could probably still beat a lot of those UFC guys. He said if I moved back to Los Angeles to fight, he would help me out. He was basically offering to manage me.

I was more interested in continuing my education than becoming a professional fighter. But I told him I would keep it in mind. Saul had this gym in Bakersfield, and I would go down there sometimes to work out and check out the other fighters.

I would also occasionally go back to Huntington Beach to party or hang out. And on one of those occasions I landed in deep shit.

I had gone to a house party in Huntington Beach with a few of my friends. Things started getting rowdy, and at one point one of my friends got hit in the face with a beer bottle by some skinhead guy. I stepped in the middle of it to defend my friend, and the skinhead tried to take me down. I got him in a choke hold while three of his friends were trying to hit me in the head with beer bottles. I kept choking the guy until he was pretty much out.

Finally, I let him go and he was unconscious. I stomped him a couple of times and then I turned around and everybody was yelling at me to leave, so I took off out the door. Then somebody called the cops. I was hiding in a bush near the house and I thought I was going to get away with it. But then a police helicopter spotted me and the cops chased me down. This one cop came up to me with his gun drawn and yelled at me to come out. It turned out that the cop with the gun was an old friend of mine named Brian Rainwater.

Friend or not, I was still taken to jail and charged with

assault with severe bodily harm. I agreed to a plea bargain of
guilty for some community service and a few days' jail time.
But I was right in the middle of training and I didn't think I
could take the time out to deal with this stuff. So I chose to
just ignore it. That's when the charge went to warrant. Suddenly I needed a lawyer and I didn't have any money.

So I turned to Tank Abbott for help. He and I weren't
getting along, but I couldn't think of anyone else to ask.

I called Tank up and asked him if he could loan me
$1,500 for an attorney, and he said no problem—he would
help me out. Well, a week went by and the attorney I hired
called me and said he needed the money. So I called Tank
and asked him if it was possible for him to get me the money
right away. I think he must have been drunk when I called
him because he said, "I ain't your fucking dad! I'm not going
to take care of you! This ain't no charity!"

I was shocked. I said, "But you said you were going to
help me out."

He said, "Fuck that!"

I was screwed.

Kristin moved up, and things were going along fine for a
while. But the wrestling coach and I were not seeing eye to
eye. He was an army brat, a real hard-ass. I could put up with
a lot of that because that kind of stuff kind of goes hand in
hand with wrestling. But what I could not deal with was that
he was very disrespectful to the kids.

David Ochoa, a longtime friend of mine, was also up in
Bakersfield and on the wrestling team. David had a real bad

stuttering problem, and still does to this day. Coach used to make fun of him. He constantly asked David questions just to make him stutter so everybody would laugh at him. I couldn't believe he was treating a student like that. If there was a purpose in humiliating him, I couldn't see it.

Coach was always playing favorites. He loved the guys who won. The guys who lost, he treated like shit.

I remember wrestling at the Midlands Championships during the third semester. It was not one of my better days. I went 3–2 in that tournament and did not place.

After the tournament, we were in a restaurant and one of our wrestlers who had won the tournament ordered a steak. That sounded good, so I ordered a steak too. Well, the food came and all of a sudden the coach was in my face, saying, "What the fuck are you eating a steak for?"

I said, "Excuse me?"

He kept at me. "What the fuck are you eating a steak for? You didn't place in the tournament."

I said, "I was hungry and a steak is what sounded good to me."

He said I didn't deserve a fucking steak. Now I was real pissed.

I got up, looked him straight in the eye, and said, "This is fucking wrong and you can have your fucking steak!" I got up, went to the bar, and ate my steak in peace. I was ready to quit the team right then and there. But I stuck it out a little bit longer. Which, in looking back on what happened next, was probably a mistake.

We had just finished a tournament in Bakersfield against Arizona, and when we got back to Bakersfield, I was having trouble with my right leg. I assumed it was what they called interior compression syndrome and didn't think a whole lot of it except that it hurt. During our next training session, when it was time to run, I told the coach I was having trouble with my leg and the pain was getting worse. Coach said, "Tape it up, you're running."

We were running up and down the gymnasium stairs that day. I got about halfway through the run and had to stop. There was just too much pain. I went to the coach and told him I couldn't run anymore.

The coach said, "Go home, you fucking pussy!"

I went back to my dorm room, and my roommate David and another friend, Raphael Davis, were there. I told them that I didn't feel good. They took one look at my legs and said they'd take me to the health center, that it didn't look good.

The people at the health center examined my legs and said, "We don't want to touch this; you're going to the emergency room."

So I went to the emergency room and the doctor told me that if I had come in two days later, they'd be chopping my leg off. It turned out that all the muscles in my leg had atrophied because of a lack of blood circulation. The doctor gave me antibiotics and told me to stay off my feet for four weeks.

I was laid up in bed for a month and the coach didn't call

once to see how I was doing. By the time I recovered, the wrestling season was over. I had been ranked second in the Pac-10 when I got injured and probably would have gone on to the Nationals. But the coach not calling was the last straw for me. I quit the team, quit school, got a U-Haul, packed my stuff, and moved back down to Huntington Beach with Kristin.

We found an apartment, and my older brother Marty helped me get a job as a clerk at Spanky's Adult Novelty Store, which was run by this cool guy named Ron Haskins. I was making fifteen dollars an hour and fifteen percent commission on anything I sold.

Working at Spanky's was nasty sometimes. I would have to chase guys out of the store who would come in to masturbate to the video and toy box covers. Girls would come in with their girlfriends and try and play with the toys. Drugged-out people would wander in and try and steal stuff. It was crazy.

Even before I started working at Spanky's, I already knew in my head that I was ready to give this fighting thing a shot. It seemed like the only thing that mattered was to keep my head straight and to dedicate myself to the sport. I figured if I gave Ultimate Fighting the same dedication I had given to high school and college wrestling, I would do pretty well.

Saul was the one who got me back into it and got my mind working. He became my first manager.

I would work at Spanky's during the day and train at

night. By all rights I should have been having my first professional, paying fight in the UFC in 1998.

But that was when Tank Abbott decided to stab me in the back.

Suddenly the UFC didn't want me and it was because Tank Abbott said he would not fight in the UFC if they used me. They wouldn't book me because of Tank, and that went on well into 1998. He carried enough weight at the time to be able to get away with that shit.

He shafted me; because of what he said, I was blackballed by the UFC. Yeah, I was angry at Tank and the UFC, but I was really frustrated because I wanted to fight. So I took my first professional fight—and this time there were no excuses.

I was fighting a totally illegal fight in a warehouse in Los Angeles. Once again, it was not sanctioned. Which meant anything could happen. And it did.

I showed up for the weigh-in and found out that the guy I was supposed to fight had dropped out of the match. I went to the promoter and told him that I really wanted to fight. The promoter said, "Well, I have this guy, Eugene Jackson."

I said "Cool. How much money will I get?" The promoter offered me $200, and I told him I'd do it.

It turned out that Eugene Jackson was no bum off the street. He was an EFC (Extreme Fighting Championship) fighter and had been some kind of Hawaiian champion. The fight lasted all of eight minutes and ended up being a draw because this was not a sanctioned UFC fight, so there were no points awarded. But I dominated that fight. In fact, I hit the guy so hard that I almost broke my hand on his face. Once again I proved to myself that I was ready for the UFC.

But thanks to Tank Abbott, the UFC still would not give me a shot. Every time I talked to Saul, he told me the same thing: "I'm calling the UFC all the time and they're not returning my calls." Finally, he suggested that we just go to a UFC event and present ourselves to the people in charge. He was convinced that would get us an in. I thought it was as good an idea as any and asked him where the next event was. Saul told me Brazil.

Ron Haskins, the owner of Spanky's, offered to sponsor us and pay our way to Brazil. So I made up these fighter cards, pictures of me along with my record, a list of who I had fought, and contact information. Saul and I went to Brazil and I presented myself to John Peretti, who was an official with the UFC. I went right up to him, gave him my card, and told him that I felt like I could beat a lot of the guys he had fighting that night. Peretti wasn't an easy sell. He wanted to know who and where I had fought. I told him I had fought twice on UFC 13, had beaten Wes Albritton, and even though I lost to Guy Mezger, I had given him an ass whipping.

Peretti would later tell me that I had come across as being very professional and that having a manager helped. He went back to the States and took a look at the tape of my fight with Mezger. Not long after we got back, Saul called me up and said he had gotten a call from the UFC. They had a fight for me.

Against my old high school opponent Jerry Bohlander.

When the fight with Jerry Bohlander was officially on, I was offered $7,500 for the fight. Now, for a former college kid who was used to getting by on Top Ramen, that was a huge amount of money. So I signed the contract without hesitation.

I began training for the fight at the Los Angeles Boxing Club. I ended up training hard for eight months because I did not want to lose.

When I wasn't thinking about fighting, I was usually thinking about the money that I could make by fighting. Growing up, I used to watch pro boxers and rock stars very closely. Many of them didn't invest their money and they didn't look out for themselves. Then a manager would take over and they would always lose out. I mean, look at Mike Tyson. That guy made $400 million and he ended up bankrupt. For me, something like that was impossible to imagine. So as I started getting into the fight game, I felt that mixed martial artists should be getting at least as big a chunk as boxers. In the beginning, I was getting decent money for a fight, but even at that point I knew I wanted more. Money was always on my mind.

I continued to train and I felt that I was in the best shape of my life. But while I was confident on the surface, I knew there was some risk involved. I could have come back to Huntington Beach, lost my first three fights, and it would have been horrible. I could have been one of the worst fighters in UFC history. But I really didn't believe that. I had enough confidence to take the chance and see what happened.

Even with the Bohlander fight coming up, I was anxious to fight and prove myself. I wanted to fight somebody right then and there. It didn't matter who.

About a month before the Bohlander fight, on December 8, 1998, I fought on a card for something called the West Coast NHB (No Holds Barred) Championships against a fighter named Jeremy Screeton. There really isn't much to say about Jeremy—he had a total of five professional fights between 1998 and 1999 and he ended up with a record of 2–3.

But as soon as it was announced that I was fighting this guy, I started getting frantic phone calls from the UFC, warning me not to fight him. They said if I lost to him, they would have to cancel my fight with Bohlander. I told them not to worry about it, that I was not going to lose.

But I was scared and intimidated the night of the fight. I really didn't know this guy, and who knew what might happen. Friends from all over Huntington Beach were in the audience, including my buddies from KoRn, as I entered the Octagon to their music.

The fight with Screeton lasted a total of sixteen seconds. He threw a punch. I threw a punch. He shot in at me in an inside cradle. I kneed him in the head a couple of times and he tapped out. I was ready for the Bohlander fight.

I saw the irony in fighting Jerry. I had beaten him years earlier in high school, and seeing him fight in the UFC was the thing that made me think that I might be good at this. And now I was fighting him again.

Jerry Bohlander was a decent fighter. At the time he was ranked top ten in the world and was in the same stable as Guy Mezger and Ken Shamrock. I was the definite underdog in the fight. To most people I was just this young kid. Then I started hearing all these interviews that Bohlander was giving. He was saying I was a nobody, that his grandmother could hit harder than I could, and that he was going to give me an ass whipping.

I thought, *We'll see whose ass gets whipped.*

The Bohlander fight took place on January 8, 1999. It was part of UFC 18: Road to the Heavyweight Title. I was pumped. The fight lasted 14 minutes, 31 seconds.

I punched him. I took him down. I punched him some more. Then I punched him some more. The referee finally stepped in and stopped the fight. Bohlander's face was cut and swollen.

Bohlander had beaten a lot of decent guys, and I had made him look pretty bad. Suddenly I was right in there with the best fighters in the middleweight division.

That was the night I earned my reputation as the Huntington Beach Bad Boy. Back in my junior college days, when I beat an opponent, I would pretend my fingers were guns, fire them, and then blow on the barrels. It was a showboating thing for sure. That's what I did that night. But I wasn't finished with my act.

Shortly before the fight, I was approached by this porno

production company called Extreme Associates. They said, "We'll pitch you a couple of grand if you wear this T-shirt after the fight."

The T-shirt said, "I Just Fucked Your Ass."

I said, "Cool, I'll do it." And my reputation was cemented.

KRISTIN ORTIZ *We blew Tito's winnings from that first fight in a few months. We went on a vacation to Cabo and we bought a lot of toys. For us, at the time, that was just an amazing amount of money.*

After the fight I went back to work at Spanky's and started partying and hitting the clubs. Everybody was giving me high fives and I was being recognized. I had some celebrity status, and it was starting to put a strain on my relationship with Kristin.

The groupies started coming around and all that. I was away a lot, and I was basically doing whatever I wanted to do. I cheated on her or I wouldn't show up at home when I told her I'd be there because I was out partying with my friends. But we were holding out for each other.

We were in love, but there was something more. We were best friends.

We had gotten through some hard times and we were going through some more hard times.

KRISTIN ORTIZ *I was nervous about the fame and what went along with it. The girls coming on to Tito. We* *had just rekindled our friendship and we were really close. I had gotten to the point where I trusted him again. Now I wasn't sure what was going to happen to us.*

After the Bohlander fight, I was pretty much out of control. I continued to work at Spanky's because the money was pretty good. By 1999, I had definitely fallen back into some bad habits and was not being very professional when it came to fighting. Basically I was on a rampage. I was partying. I was smoking pot, doing a little crystal meth, and drinking a lot. I wasn't an alcoholic, but I would party nonstop, drinking every day. It was fun for me. It was my getaway.

But while I was still a loose cannon when it came to my personal life, my attitude toward being a professional wrestler, despite my best efforts to the contrary, was maturing. I had loved Tank Abbott like a brother at one point. But when he refused to help me out, that was the end between us. Besides, I felt it was time to grow and become a better fighter by learning from others. I went to train with another wrestler, John, who was very good with submission holds. He was a good addition to my training team, and he worked me real hard.

But what I had yet to learn was that fighters had egos and feelings. Respect was an important element of a fighter's makeup. And any perception of disrespect could have dire consequences. I learned this the hard way when it came to John.

John had fought Frank Shamrock around this time and had been pretty much dominated. Not long after his fight, we had gone out partying and drinking and getting really wasted. At one point in the evening, I went up to John and told him I thought I could beat Frank Shamrock. I wasn't trying to be disrespectful to John or to put him down. But I honestly thought that I had more to give in a Frank Shamrock fight than John did. But I think I may have hurt his feelings, because things started to get a bit strained between us.

Right in the middle of my renewed dedication to the sport, I got a call from the UFC. Vitor Belfort had been scheduled to fight Guy Mezger, but he had to pull out at the last minute. They wanted me to fill in and fight Mezger. I hadn't been training much and I wasn't really in shape, but my manager said he was sure I could beat this guy. And up to this point, I had to admit, Saul had not steered me wrong, so I agreed to do it.

So I jumped back into training full-on three weeks before the fight and hoped for the best. I put my running shoes on and ran for a week. I sparred a little bit. It was kind of a payback thing. Mezger had beaten me before I turned pro and before I really knew a lot about the fight game. But I had always felt that I had been robbed in that match. Now that I was doing this for real, for money, I really wanted to beat this guy. I wanted payback.

I fought Guy Mezger on March 5, 1999, in the event titled UFC 19: Ultimate Young Guns. From the opening bell I just bombarded him. I hit him with everything, and the referee stopped it thirteen minutes into the fight. I had another shirt ready for the occasion.

It read: "Gay Mezger Is My Bitch."

Mezger had talked a lot of shit, put his foot in his mouth, and then couldn't pull it out. So when it was over and done with, I felt justified in wearing the shirt.

But I was still a young kid and I got caught up in the moment. I flipped off Guy Mezger and I flipped off his corner. Ken Shamrock was in his corner. Looking back on it, I would have to say that flipping off Shamrock was probably the beginning of our feud.

The crowd went wild, but I would get a lot of heat for it later. I didn't realize it at the time, but I probably pissed off a lot of fighters that night. Ken Shamrock was really pissed off. His attitude was, "Who is this fucking kid?" But I knew who I was.

I wasn't really aware of the image I was projecting. I was interviewed after the fight, and the interviewer asked me if Mezger should be mad about the shirt. I said of course he should be mad. Then I kind of threw down a challenge when I said, "And Ken Shamrock should be mad too. I just beat his number one and two guys back-to-back."

I was following the way Tank Abbott went about his business—he talked a lot of shit, but then he backed it up when he fought. I felt like that's what I was doing.

But I have to admit that this character I had become was all very new to me. I didn't really know who this character was, but I kind of liked him.

I liked being the bad boy.

CHAPTER NINE

Fighting Mad

*H*igh on wins, I wanted a shot at the UFC title.

Yeah, I may have been a little arrogant. After all, I had only had three professional fights. But even at that point, I thought I was one of the best in the business. I wanted to take on the champ. I wanted Frank Shamrock.

And the trash talking had already begun.

We ran into each other at a UFC event, and I walked right up to him and told him that I would love to fight him and take his belt away. Frank said, "Yeah, whatever, kid. You never will." All of a sudden the UFC gets in the middle of all our talk and says that there's going to be a title fight.

People outside the business thought that fighters were making big money. But the reality was that when I signed the contract to fight Shamrock for the championship, I was getting $25,000 for the fight. And for fighters at that time, that was good money. But the money really wasn't the most important thing to me. I fought for the love of fighting and for the attention that I never got as a kid.

I was stoked to be fighting for the title, and I immediately got into a real hard-core level of training. But I still didn't understand what it meant to train on a professional level, and that training would have to be my job for the next three months. I was training as hard as I knew how. A little more than a month before the fight I thought, *Well, I've been working my ass off. I think I'll take a couple of days off.*

So I went down to Mexico for a couple of days with a friend of mine to do some fishing. While I was there, I was also drinking a lot and smoking pot. It was still six weeks out from the fight with Shamrock, and I didn't think it was going to hurt me. I came back and got right back into training. I felt I had prepared myself well for the fight.

This was around the time that my relationship with John began to get even more strained. I had never used steroids or performance-enhancing drugs of any kind and had no interest in doing so. I was a firm believer in developing my body naturally. But as the fight with Frank Shamrock got closer, John was encouraging me to take steroids and insisting that they would give me the edge in a fight with Shamrock. I kept saying no, and he was upset that I wouldn't take them. Needless to say, our relationship at that point was not good.

The "There Can Only Be One Champion" fight between Frank Shamrock and me took place on September 24, 1999. I came into the fight thinking I was just going to bulldoze him. And I'd like to think that for the first three rounds I did.

When the fight started, I was dominating him, taking him down and beating him down. But by the fourth round my stamina just went out the door. I had been giving a hundred percent from the start and I just got fatigued. I had pushed and pushed and pushed, and then I didn't have anything left. I think if I had relaxed a bit during the course of the fight I would have beaten him. But I was new to all this and had just decided to go hard the whole way.

It was during the Shamrock fight that I discovered that John had decided to get even with me for my perceived disrespect for him by hanging me out to dry. John was my cornerman, but during the fight, he never said a thing to me. He never told me how much time was left and he told everybody else in the corner to be quiet and not to say anything. He really left me to go out there and fight by myself.

Shamrock was a pro who had defended his title five times already, and he knew just how to take the wind out of me. In the fourth round, he caught me with a choke hold. I got out of it. Then he hit me in the back of the head and I couldn't defend myself, so I tapped out.

Of course, I had a Frank Shamrock T-shirt all ready to go. I had met him a couple of months earlier and had him sign it.

And when he beat me, I put it on and walked around the ring in it. He had beaten me fair and square. But in some ways that loss was like a win for me because I came out of the fight realizing that in the future I would have to pace myself.

Losing that match brought me crashing back to earth. I just couldn't believe I had lost. My trainers told me I had done a good job, but I was bummed. All I could think of was that I had lost my chance to be world champion.

The sad thing was that I decided to let John go after that fight. His pushing the steroids was part of the problem, but it basically boiled down to not being able to trust the guy anymore.

Right after the Shamrock fight, Saul Garcia and I also parted company. What it came down to was that Saul was in over his head. Yeah, he got me a couple of fights when I first started, but I was basically doing a lot of the work myself.

As far as I was concerned, Saul was making bad business decisions and costing me money. When I fought Frank Shamrock, I was supposed to get $25,000. I only got $10,000. After signing the contract, I found out that the UFC said they were cutting my fee and Saul didn't have the balls to go up against them. When I saw that, I said this isn't going to happen again.

The split was amicable at the beginning. But then I found out that Saul had gone out and made a DVD that said that he had made my career. He claimed that he was the one who told me to bleach my hair and to start wearing the T-shirts. The guy was just full of shit. He was telling nothing but lies, and I had to spend a lot of time in interviews disputing all the things he said.

Some good did actually come out of the fight with Shamrock, though. That fight put me on a course to my first non-fighting business venture.

After the fight a kid came up to me and asked if I had a T-shirt for sale that had my name on it. I told him I didn't, but I thought about it afterward and it sounded like a pretty good idea. So I went home and got together with my brother Marty. He was raving about the punishment I had given Shamrock, and the word "punishment" kind of stuck in my head. I looked up the definition of the word and found that "to punish" meant to threaten or cause severe damage. So I got the idea to put the word "Punishment" on a T-shirt with TitoOrtiz.com under it. I kicked in $500 to get it going, and we printed the T-shirts on a silk-screen machine my brother Marty had in his garage. Kristin understood the business and marketing side of things, and she stepped in to help. I started selling T-shirts, and within the first year, we cleared quite a bit.

Not long after the shirts began selling, I decided to expand the line to include a version of the flame shorts I fought in. The first ones we made didn't really look very good, but they sold. That was pretty much the moment Punishment Athletic Wear was born. I gave Kristin fifty-percent ownership in the company. I was doing my own thing, and the money I was making off the shirts and shorts was like icing on the cake.

After taking a couple of days off to wind down from the Shamrock fight, I went back to work at Spanky's. As soon as I walked into the office, the boss asked me to have a seat. He said flat out, "I don't think this job is for you."

I said, "Fighting? I love fighting!"

He said "No, I mean working here. I think there's something better for you out there."

I thought I was being fired.

Then he said, "You do what you need to do to get your work in and I'll pay for your rent and your cell phone, and give you a per diem for six months." The only condition was that I had to put "Spanky's" on my shorts and he even gave me extra money for that.

I got back into training full on. And there was only one thing I was training for—a rematch with Frank Shamrock. I wanted that rematch badly. So did the UFC. As it turned out, the only person who didn't was Frank Shamrock.

Shamrock said the money wasn't good enough for him to fight me. So he gave up his title and retired. That left the title vacant. I felt I would be in line to fight for it at some point, so I knew I'd better be in good shape when the call came. And I figured the best way to learn was from somebody who beat me, so I called Frank Shamrock and asked him if I could come up and train with him. He said sure.

I trained with him for a couple of weeks and I got to see what it took to be a top contender. He taught me a lot about cardio and the importance of rest and recovery time. I watched tapes of his fights and saw that he could be super dangerous.

Around that time I received a phone call from some people in the United Arab Emirates who were putting on something called the World Submissions Championships in Abu Dhabi. It was a competition in which no strikes were involved, just wrestling submissions. I was a big enough name that they invited me to compete, but they figured I wouldn't do well because this match was just about wrestling and not about striking. What they didn't realize was that I was good at submissions.

I also realized that there would be a time difference to overcome, so I changed my training schedule before I went overseas. Normally my workouts would start early, like around four in the morning. But before I went to Abu Dhabi I did all my training around midnight, which would allow me to adjust to the time change when I was there.

I went and took third in my weight and took fourth in the absolutes, which was all the weights combined. It was a confidence builder. I won four of my five fights against some really good fighters and I showed a lot of people that I could beat world-class fighters with submission holds rather than just going to the ground and pounding. None of this counted on my professional record, but I did end up making $16,000 in cash.

I had never been out of the country before, so being in the Middle East was a surreal experience for me. The people, the culture—I had never experienced anything like that in my life.

While I was in the Middle East I ran into this UFC matchmaker named Joe Silva, who had come over to check out fighters. He told me that the UFC wanted me to fight this guy named Wanderlei Silva.

I knew who Silva was, and he was a badass. He had this intimidating stare. The story going around was that a lot of guys didn't want to fight him because they were afraid of him. He fought with the Pride organization in Japan, and he was from Brazil. Joe Silva told me that he thought I could beat him. He also said that this fight was for Shamrock's vacant title and that if I wanted the fight, it was mine.

I had to think about it for a minute. For some reason, I wasn't really sure if I wanted the fight. Then I said, "Fuck it, I'll do it." I signed for the fight and started training again.

I trained for four solid months, and this time I took it seriously. There were no drugs. I brought a lot of guys in to train with me, people like Chuck Liddell and John Lewis.

It was during this training period that Team Punishment was formed. It wasn't really that big a deal. Chuck Liddell and I had been training together for a while, and we just decided one day that we needed a name for our team. One of my brothers suggested "Team Punishment," and we got Ricco Rodriguez, John Lewis, and Rampage to join us.

Over the years, different people trained under the team name. They would be introduced as being from Team Punishment when they fought, but it has always been for training and social purposes more than anything else. It's kind of like being in a gang without the bad stuff . . . except when Team Punishment members get in the Octagon.

But it was not as simple as all that. Trouble was right around the corner.

At that point that whole mess with that old fight warrant caught up with me.

Somebody at the UFC suggested that I go to Las Vegas

for a couple of months and hide out. He said that I could use the excuse that I was going to Vegas to do some promotion for a UFC-Pride fight. But the reality was that there was a warrant out for my arrest. If I had stayed in Los Angeles and got pulled over for something stupid, all they had to do was run my name and I would be going to jail. So I went to Las Vegas and trained for a couple of months, and nobody found me. After a couple of months, I came back to Los Angeles, Kristin's parents loaned me the money for the lawyer, and I dealt with it.

The fight with Wanderlei Silva took place on April 4, 2000, in Japan. This was my time to shine. I was not going to back down. I was ready to go to war. The fight was billed as UFC 25: Ultimate Japan 3. And from the opening bell, I was in control of the match.

I took him down and dominated on top. In the third round he did hit me with a punch that dropped me, but I got right back on my feet and took him down. At the end of the match, I had taken a five-round decision.

My victory shirt for that fight read: "I Just Killed an Axe Murderer."

After a year and a half of professional fighting, I was now the lightweight champion of the world. I swear, when they announced that I had won, I had an out-of-body experience. I had come to realize that all the hard work and determination I had put into this sport had resulted in my becoming the best fighter in the world.

I thought, *Wow! This is really happening!*

JOYCE ROBLES *When I found out that Tito was fighting for a living, I was scared to death. I didn't like the idea of anyone hitting my son.*

When I came back from Japan, I slept with that belt for at least a month. I knew I had succeeded. I had worked hard and had gotten the ultimate prize.

It was at this point that Dana White came into my life.

One of my trainers at the time, John Lewis, had been training Dana White in jujitsu. Dana was a huge fan of the sport and had watched me fight a lot. John and Dana were talking one day, and the subject of who was managing me came up. By that time Saul and I had called it quits, and for all intents and purposes, I was managing myself. Dana wanted to know what he could do to get me to let him manage me.

Dana and I arranged a meeting. John introduced us, and we just started talking. He told me that he had worked with Floyd Mayweather Jr. and a lot of boxers, that he kind of knew the business, and that he thought he could help me out.

At that point I was a bit skeptical. I felt that anybody who talked to me about money was full of shit. I really didn't know what to think. Then Dana called again and said, "I want to come down to Huntington Beach and sit down with you and do this deal." He said he was signing Chuck Liddell as well and that he was anxious to bring me on board. I still wasn't sure. But then a friend of mine whose opinion I respected, Wayne Harriman, said that Dana was a really good guy and that I should go with him.

So Dana flew down and came knocking on my door. He sat me down and asked me what I wanted to do with my future. Then he described how he was going to help me and basically promised me the world. I asked Kristin what she thought, and she said that it sounded like a good deal. So I signed up with Dana to manage me.

Now that I was world champion, there was a lot of press and media interest in me. And, of course, I loved the attention. But I don't think Kristin did.

I remember one night we had gone to see a show at the House of Blues in Hollywood. After the show I was surrounded by all kinds of people wanting to get autographs, have pictures taken, and do interviews. Kristin was standing off to the side, essentially being ignored by everybody, including me. Every once in a while she'd come up to me and say, "Let's go home and go to bed." But I would stay until everybody that had come up to me had been taken care of. I've always been an outgoing kind of person, and when people are giving you all this attention, you want to suck up as much of it as possible—at any cost.

KRISTIN ORTIZ *There were so many incidents like that night at the House of Blues. Fans tended to look at Tito like he was God and not a real person. And nobody knew who I was. I was always getting knocked over and pushed out of the way. That's just the way people are when they see somebody like Tito. It was exhausting being around him in public because he always had to be on.*

Kristin was helping me out quite a bit; she was handling a lot of my business and helping to pay taxes. And I needed the help because I wasn't making a lot of money, despite the fact that I was a champion. Even though Ultimate Fighting was evolving and reaching more and more people, the public perception was that it was a barbaric sport, stuck in the Dark Ages. Ultimate Fighters were considered crazy guys who did crazy shit.

Luckily my manager, Dana White, knew how to negotiate. He knew how to push without pushing too hard, and he wouldn't budge on the important deal points. When it all came down, I had a great new contract, which was surprising, considering there wasn't any pay-per-view back then and UFC merchandising was almost nonexistent. Before Dana, I was making maybe $50,000 tops for a fight. With my new contract, I was making $80,000 to $100,000 per fight.

Less than a year after Dana took over as my manager, there was a big change in the UFC.

The Fertitta brothers had been following the organization's progress for a while and they recognized its potential— potential that was not being realized with Bob Meyerwitz at the helm. Bob was tired of the grind and was ready to sell, so the Fertittas bought the UFC from him for $4 million and then put about $25 million into the organization.

The impact on the fighters and the UFC was immediate. I was bound by my existing contract, but now I was flying in Learjets and staying in presidential suites . . . and loving every minute of it.

And, as always, I slipped right back into my crazy ways after winning the championship—running around, disappearing for days on end, and partying real hard, which was putting a real strain on Kristin and on our relationship.

We had been together for quite a while, and Kristin really didn't want to do the single thing anymore. So she gave me a choice: either marry her or leave her. I didn't want to lose Kristin because she was a really good girl and I cared about her deeply. But we were arguing a lot more and it was taking a toll on me. All the same, I still went out and bought a ring, and I was getting ready to take that step.

KRISTIN ORTIZ *Our relationship was on the rocks. There were all these red flags that Tito was not being faithful, but I was young and naïve and I didn't want to believe it. Even if he was cheating, I didn't want to lose my best friend and so I didn't really want to know. He was always a good liar and I believed him.*

One night I came home and Kristin started in on me. She was yelling and crying and we really got into it. And then, right in the middle of this wicked fight, I looked at Kristin and thought, *I really love this girl.* All of a sudden it just came out. I went to the bathroom and came out with the ring.

I said, "Will you marry me?"

And just like that, we were engaged.

CHAPTER TEN

Hello from Bermuda

We were married in Huntington Beach in June 2000.

KRISTIN ORTIZ   *The wedding was amazing. We wrote and recited our own vows. Tito cried. But then, Tito cries a lot. The idea that we were getting married really got to him. He's just this big, emotional guy.*

I had finally made my love for Kristin official, and I felt really good about it. We left for our honeymoon in Bermuda on June 25. The first day there we were watching people riding all over the place on these mopeds and it looked like a lot of fun. The next morning Kristin and I decided to rent a moped, and we spent a good part of the day driving around, doing all the tourist stuff. We were on our way back to the hotel in the afternoon when we got to a stop sign. It was a two-way stop at a three-way intersection. I came to a stop. A car went by. Another car was coming from the other direction and stopped. The driver waved me to go ahead. I looked left and pulled out.

Boom!

Right before the crash, Kristin yelled at me to watch out.

Then the bus hit us. It had to have been going thirty miles an hour, and the impact threw me about twenty feet in the air. I hit the ground, rolled, and slid right into oncoming traffic. I remember lying there, screaming at the traffic to stop.

Kristin was caught underneath the bus, and it dragged her for about eight feet before it stopped. The bus tire was about three inches from her head. I yelled, "Kristin, are you okay?" When she said no, I flipped out. I got up and went to grab her when a lady yelled and told me not to touch her. I was dizzy, my head was spinning. I sat down and fell over. I got up and went to Kristin. An ambulance had arrived and they were trying to pull her out from under the bus. She was saying that her back hurt. Then one of the ambulance guys looked at me and said, "Oh my God! Are you okay?"

I had road rash all up and down the left side of my body. I looked over to where the bus had stopped, and there was my body print on the bus. The ambulance took us to the emergency room. I was a mess, but Kristin was a lot worse.

She had crushed one of her vertebrae, fractured four others, broken three ribs, and had road rash all over her body.

It was the first day of our honeymoon, and we were lucky to be alive.

I was trembling. I was scared. I thought I had lost her. I was just thankful that somebody was looking out for me and that they didn't take Kristin's or my life away. I had thought of myself as the toughest man in the world. But there I was, standing on the road, scared like a little kid.

We were in the hospital for three days, and I didn't sleep the entire time. After three days we arranged for a private jet to pick us up in Bermuda and take us back to the States. Kristin was strapped into a gurney on the plane. During the flight she said, "I'm glad we're okay."

I smiled. "I'm glad we're okay too."

All of a sudden the plane started shaking. We looked out the window and there was a thunderstorm on the left side of the plane. Kristin started crying. She said, "I don't want to die in a plane crash."

I said, "We just got hit by a fucking bus. If it was our turn to die, we'd be dead by now."

We landed safely, and when we got back to Orange County, Kristin was in a back brace for six months. I cried every time I saw her like that. I felt like the whole accident was completely my fault because I hadn't been paying attention. I really took it hard. I could barely get myself to train even a little bit. I was depressed. Plus the wounds I had were so bad that I basically had to take two months off to let them heal.

KRISTIN ORTIZ   *After the accident we moved in with my parents. It was a rough time for Tito. He was dealing with the guilt of what had happened. Tito had a hard time dealing with a lot of situations. He was not a big communicator. Sometimes he would just plain disconnect from situations and all you would get is a blank stare. He was coping with a lot, and all he really wanted to do was run away.*

During the time that Kristin and I were married and, literally, recovering from our honeymoon, a lot had changed. After the Fertittas had bought the UFC, the talk was that John Lewis would become the new UFC president. But the next thing I heard was that Dana had swooped in and taken the job right out from under him. Personally I thought it was a cheap move on Dana's part. He called to tell me that he'd just been named president of the UFC and that he couldn't be my manager anymore because it would be a conflict of interest.

At the time, we were working with an attorney named James Gallow, and Dana told me he was going to appoint him as my new manager. This didn't sound quite right to me. I told Dana, "Well, Gallow's an attorney. He knows nothing about managing. How is he going to take over for you?" Dana said not to worry; everything was going to be fine.

I trusted Dana. I trusted him without a doubt. I wasn't the most business-savvy guy, but I felt everybody was looking out for my best interests. So I agreed to let James manage me. However, in the back of my mind, I was thinking there was still a conflict of interest.

Nevertheless, I said yes and got back to fighting.

Not long after we returned from Bermuda, I got a phone call from the UFC. They asked me when I wanted to fight again. I needed the money real bad, so I said I would defend my title. It was July when they called and they wanted me to fight in December. I was to fight Yuki Kondo in his homeland, Japan. I knew immediately that this fight wasn't going to be easy.

Yuki Kondo was the king of rings, a very good fighter. He had beaten Frank Shamrock. He was capable of taking everything I could give him punchingwise. I knew I was going to have to get a submission hold on him, because that was the only way I was going to stop him.

I started training in September, and I was taking it very seriously. I felt bad about leaving Kristin even for a little bit to train, but by that time she was beginning to recover. She was going through hell and yet she was sucking it up. I figured I had to do the same.

I remember liking Japan immediately. The country was so nice and clean. There was no graffiti, no trash. It was just a very clean environment. I felt out of place there, but I kept it together by focusing on the task at hand.

Which was to impose my will on Yuki Kondo.

The fight was simply billed as UFC 29: Defense of the Belts. The arena was packed with people screaming and hollering. It was obvious that Kondo was the fan favorite. But I did get my share of the applause when I came down to the cage.

I remember the announcer rattling off a bunch of Japanese and then saying, "Yuki Kondo." Then he rattled off some more Japanese and said, "The Millennium Bad Boy, Tito Ortiz." The audience responded with loud cheers and I remember thinking how cool it was to get such a great reaction from this crowd in Japan.

The fight was close for about the first minute and a half. I came out at the bell, threw a right hand, and missed. He slipped. I went to go shoot and he threw a flying knee that clipped me right on the chin. I fell back, rolled up to my feet, and body-locked him.

I don't remember saying it, but the referee, John McCarthy, told me later that when I grabbed him, I was yelling at him, "Is that all you've got?" I picked him up off the ground, slammed him on the floor, and just beat on him with punches and elbows. He tried to shoot to my legs and I grabbed him with a cobra choke, one of my best submission moves. I torqued it. He couldn't breathe, and then he tapped out.

The fight had lasted less than two minutes and I was still the world champion.

I reached for my victory shirt and put it on. I'm not sure if the Japanese quite understood what the shirt thing was all about, but this one read: "RESPECT I don't earn it I just fucken take it."

The whole celebrity thing was at an even higher level after the Kondo fight. When I returned to the States, I would love to say that I stopped the heavy partying and the cheating. But every once in a while I would go out, get drunk, and something would happen. I don't know if Kristin knew for sure what was going on, but I think she sensed it.

KRISTIN ORTIZ *Tito was traveling all the time, he was gone a lot. I didn't see him much, and even when he did come back, he would be training. If I had issues, I couldn't talk about them with him because he was in training mode. Once he was done fighting, it was all about him having fun and partying. All of a sudden it was never about me.*

The whole celebrity thing was at an even higher level after the Kondo fight. It was even more about me and less about her. The impact of my celebrity was definitely starting to weigh on Kristin, and she started complaining about it. She sat me down a few times and told me, "Tito, I didn't marry you because you were going to be a superstar. I married the Tito who was the nice guy and who was nice to me. All of a sudden you're becoming a superstar and so many people are giving you so much attention. It seems like you don't have enough time for me."

She was right. Things were changing. Personally and professionally.

The new owners of the UFC wanted me to fight again, and fairly soon. They were so anxious to make this happen that they were willing to pay for my training camp up in Big Bear, California. The guy they wanted me to fight was Evan Tanner. He was a former middleweight champion and a real tough guy.

So I went up to Big Bear. I brought Chuck Liddell and a bunch of other guys with me. I must have had fifteen guys up there at one point. It was only about a two-month training period, but I worked real hard, and because it had been so close to the Kondo fight, I felt I was in really good shape.

The fight with Evan Tanner was held on February 23, 2001, and was billed as UFC 30: Battle on the Boardwalk. The fight only lasted thirty seconds, but it was a pretty brutal one. I kicked him. He tried to clinch and grab ahold of me. I clinched his head. I kneed him in the belly and uppercut him to the face. Finally I picked him up and drilled him into the floor. The impact knocked him out. He was unconscious for about seven minutes.

I put on a shirt that said: "If You Can Read This I Just Stomped His Ass!"

By this time my relationship with Kristin was pretty rocky. I continued to cheat on her and I wasn't being real discreet about it.

And at that point I really didn't care if she found out. Cheating was a big mistake on my part, but subconsciously, I guess I wanted to get caught.

Kristin was desperate to save the marriage, and she felt that having a kid would do that. I wasn't sure. I didn't want to make the same mistakes my parents had made. But we continued to talk about it. And the more we talked, the more it began sounding like a good idea.

KRISTIN ORTIZ *When we first got married, Tito told me he wanted four kids. He wanted to get me pregnant right away. I was the one saying, "Whoa! Let's take some time first." After his career started to boom and he started making money, I was settled at home and ready to have a kid. Now he was the one saying, "Let's wait, let's wait." We kept talking about it and finally we both decided that we wanted a baby. But looking back on that time, I could see it in his eyes. There was something wrong. He had reservations, but he did it to make me happy.*

The idea of starting a family really scared me. And I know it had a lot to do with how my parents neglected me when I was growing up. I would see my mother once in a while, but I had pretty much cut off all communication with my father. To be honest, I still hated them both for what they had put me through.

But a lot of the hostility toward my mother faded when she sent me this long handwritten letter on my twenty-fifth birthday. She told me why things had turned out the way they had and she told me how sorry she was for the way things had gone for me. It took a brave person to do what

Tito checking out the world at age one.

Joyce is all smiles as newborn Tito naps.

Tito's parents, Samuel and Joyce, hard at work taking
the leaves off marijuana plants.

Tito, age five, flanked by older brothers Mike, Marty,
and Tiger the dog.

Tito, age four, on the beach at Corona Del Mar, California.

JOHN R. PETERSON SCHOOL
Huntington Beach, California
1980-81
MRS. CONNIE WAKEFIELD
Principal

MRS. TIMOTHY
KINDERGARTEN P.M.

Tito's kindergarten class photo. That's Tito on the far right, top row.

Tito in a hard-fought match with Rico Martinez during his sophomore year in high school.

Tito on top during a junior college wrestling tournament.

Tito's high school wrestling team photo. Tito is in the first row, dead in the middle.

Tito graduates high school. Brothers Mike and Jim can't believe it.

Tito and his mom celebrate after Tito captured his first world title. Tito was twenty-three at the time.

Tito and former wife Kristin are all smiles during a pre-fight dinner.

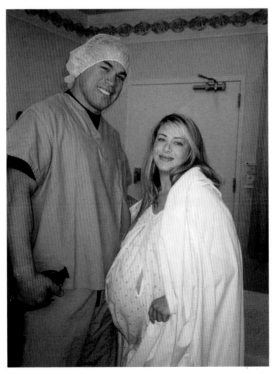

A very big Tito and a very big Kristin just hours before the birth of their son, Jacob.

Tito sharing a quiet
moment with then
six-month-old Jacob.

Tito and Jacob show off
their matching Mohawks.

Jacob brings out the
smiles in papa Tito.

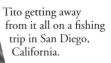

Tito getting away
from it all on a fishing
trip in San Diego,
California.

Tito poses proudly with the catch
of the day. It's a simple equation:
bigger man lands bigger fish.

Tito proves
that he is
a two-fisted
fisherman with
an albacore in
each hand.

Tito and Jacob strike a menacing pose. Like father, like son.

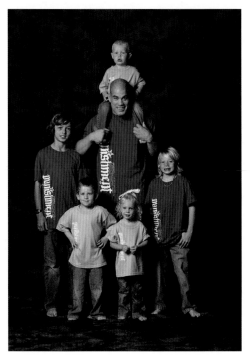

Tito is a kid magnet during a photo shoot for his Punishment clothing line.

Fighters on the prowl in Japan. From left: Shone Carter, Chris Liddell, Tito, Chuck Liddell.

Jenna Jameson kicks Tito's ass.

Tito and Jenna contemplate love, not war.

Tito Ortiz: The scariest man on the planet.

Tito strikes a pounding pose during a recent photo shoot.

Tito gets his fight face on
during a recent photo session.

Tito's shirts tell the tales of victories over Jerry Bohlander (top left), Patrick Côté (top right), Chuck Liddell (bottom left), and Ken Shamrock (bottom right).

Tito strikes a bad-boy pose.

my mother did and a strong person to make the choices she made so her kids could survive.

JOYCE ROBLES *The letter I sent Tito told him how I met his father and how and why things had turned out the way they did. I really poured my heart out to him.*

Around that time, the UFC was really moving in a new direction. There were more rules and more clearly defined weight classifications. The sport was growing in popularity, and, whether they wanted to admit it or not, I was one of the main reasons for that growth. I had become this flamboyant, charismatic, larger-than-life character, which was what the sport needed. I was also real big on promotion. Unlike a lot of the fighters, I was articulate and media savvy. Yeah, I was full of myself and I talked a lot of shit, but I felt I had the goods to back it up.

Unfortunately, by 2001 I began to think I had made a mistake in agreeing with Dana about James Gallow being my manager. All of a sudden I was flying coach again and I wasn't staying in the presidential suite anymore. I had signed a contract and I was sticking to it, but I began asking for little things, things that on the surface were not that big a deal, but as champ, I felt I deserved them.

Jim was not even close to the hard-charging manager Dana had been. He would tell me, "We shouldn't be asking for things like that. We don't want to get Dana mad. Let's not ask for more. We should be happy with what we're getting now."

When I started hearing stuff like that, I realized that Jim wasn't really looking out for my best interests but rather for the best interests of the UFC. Every time I asked him for something, he would make out like I was busting his balls. I finally called him on it and said, "Aren't you supposed to be looking out for my best interests?" He assured me that he was, but I soon discovered the real nature of the relationship between Dana and Jim. Things were smooth between them because every time Jim would ask for something, Dana would tell him, "Fuck you! I got you here. If it wasn't for me, you wouldn't be here right now." That was their relationship, and I was getting screwed because of it.

I was the one out there promoting the sport and the UFC. I wasn't like Chuck Liddell, who had two-word answers to everything. I answered every question that was put to me. I didn't shy away from the press like most of the other fighters did. I was the flag bearer for the sport, and I felt I deserved a little more money because I was working harder than anybody else. And I finally got so frustrated that I told Dana that.

His response was, "Yeah, you're the champ, but we're still not making very much money."

I told him, "Well, when the time comes and the UFC is making some money, then I want to start making more money."

I was still pissed, but I let it go for the time being and got back to business.

The UFC did, as well, which is why they continued to

exploit my popularity. Not too long after the Tanner fight, they asked me to defend my title again. This time against a fighter named Elvis Sinosic.

So it was back up to Big Bear and a solid six weeks of training in preparation for that fight. The main reason I go there is to get away from the city. A lot of fighters tend to take things for granted when they are living their normal lives. When I train in Big Bear, I don't have any fun at all. There's nowhere to go up there and friends can't come over to visit. All I do is eat, sleep, and train.

I fought Sinosic on June 29, 2001, in a match that was billed as UFC 32: Showdown in the Meadowlands. He was a good fighter, but he was just too skinny. He hit me with a punch at one point and I was dazed for a second. Then I took him to the ground and I just pounded him out. I stopped him in less than three minutes in the first round.

More press. More media attention. More partying. And yes, occasionally, more women. It was nonstop, and I was soaking it all up like a sponge. The UFC stepped in with yet another deal in place. It went without saying that the money was real good at this point. It also went without saying that the time between fights was getting shorter and shorter. But I was a young kid who really loved to fight, so I wasn't too concerned.

My next fight was with Vladimir Matyushenko. He was a Russian Olympic wrestler. The buzz was building that this might be a tougher fight than anybody expected and that I might get outwrestled by this guy. There was this kind of

Rocky vibe going on, an us-versus-them kind of thing. The fight with Matyushenko was turning into a big deal.

So I went back up to Big Bear and started training real hard. I knew I had the chops to outwrestle this guy, but I put in a little extra time with Chuck Liddell and some of the other guys I was training with.

At some point near the end of training, Kristin came up to visit me. We were still talking constantly about having a baby. Well, one thing led to another and we ended up having sex. It was just one time and then she left. I went back to training.

I went to bed early on September 10, 2001.

When I woke up the next morning I found out that the whole world had changed.

Forever.

CHAPTER ELEVEN

9/11

I was sound asleep in my bed in Big Bear, California, when the first plane hit.

One of my trainers came in and said, "Tito, get up, man! You've got to see what's happening!" It was easily about four hours before I normally got up, so I told him to leave me alone and to let me sleep. But he insisted that I get up. Finally I got up, thinking this had better be really important.

I walked into the next room where there was a television going. What I saw was the New York skyline and a building on fire. There were shots of people running in the street. Then I saw the second plane fly into the second building and explode. I was shocked and in total disbelief.

I watched the buildings crumble and people jump to their deaths. I was stunned that something like this could be happening in America.

The worst attack on American soil in modern history

was unfolding before my very eyes. Not too surprisingly, my phone started ringing off the hook.

Immediately people from the UFC started calling and saying that the right thing to do would be to cancel the fight with Matyushenko, which was to take place on September 28. I said no way.

First of all I needed the money and the arena had already sold out all thirteen thousand seats. But I also felt that with all that had just happened, Americans would need this kind of fight to raise their spirits. People needed something, anything, to unite them, and I felt strongly that this fight would help people begin to get over this horrible situation and to begin the healing process.

So the fight was not canceled.

That same day, I received a telephone call from Kristin. She was pregnant.

KRISTIN ORTIZ *Tito didn't want to lose me, which is why I think he finally agreed that we should have a baby. He figured having a baby would make me happy and that the baby would give me something to do while he was out running amuck.*

I was excited. I was stoked. I was happy. But then all of a sudden the full impact of fatherhood hit me. *I'm going to be a dad now? Am I going to be able to do it? I mean, look at what a lousy job my dad did.* All of that stuff from the past came rushing back to me, and I was starting to second-guess myself.

Money had always been an issue for me. And making money had always been very important to me. Suddenly, with fatherhood on the way, it was even more important than ever.

I wanted to make sure that I made enough money to support my family and to support my child. I wanted to make sure that my kid didn't have to steal and grow up in motels and cars and see all the stuff I had seen at a young age. It was so hard for me growing up that I decided my kid deserved to be spoiled.

All of which meant I had to make even more money than I was making now. Which meant that at some point I would have to do other things. But for now it was all about fighting—and that meant taking care of Matyushenko.

The fight with Matyushenko was billed as UFC 33: Victory in Vegas. The entire arena was rocking. I came into the ring carrying an American flag. My entrance music that night was the song "Break Stuff" by the band Limp Bizkit. Everybody was going crazy. People were screaming "USA! USA!" I felt so great that this fight was taking place.

I dominated from the opening bell and won a unanimous five-round decision.

The next few months were all about Kristin. The pregnancy was going along well. Kristin gained sixty pounds; she had cut out the soda and the junk food and was taking a lot of vitamins. And I was there for her constantly. It was beginning to look like things might work out for Kristin and me.

But then the bad habits returned.

I met a stripper named Heather in Las Vegas.

I was in Vegas getting ready to go to Japan to help promote a Pride fighting event. I was hanging out at the strip club where she worked, and I hid my ring, of course, so she wouldn't know that I was married. We got together. I hung out with her. Then I went to Japan. Then I came back to Vegas and hung out with her some more. Heather was a very beautiful girl, and she was very interested in me.

At that point, being beautiful and interested was all it took.

I would go home for a while and then I would go back to Vegas. Before I knew it I was having a full-blown affair that ultimately ended up lasting four years. All of a sudden I was leading a double life. For all the cheating I had done, this affair was the most serious. And I was doing it while my wife, Kristin, was carrying my child.

KRISTIN ORTIZ *I was about seven months pregnant. This was really a hard time. Tito was home. And everything suddenly seemed to be bugging him.*

My son Jacob was born on June 1, 2002. He was delivered by C-section. I cried the first time I saw my son in the hospital. I was the first one to hold him. It was such a joyous feeling that I can't even begin to describe my emotions at that moment. He just opened his eyes and looked at me. When they pulled him out and handed him to me, I think I said, "Oh my God, he's so beautiful" about fifty times. It was so amazing. Until you have a kid, you don't know what love really is.

After Jacob was born, I have to admit that I started getting a little paranoid. I knew that financially I had to do my job, but as a father, I was really scared. I didn't want to make mistakes. I didn't want to hurt him. I didn't want to take him places because I was afraid that something might happen to him. I wanted to protect him as much as possible. For a long time, I was crazy with fear.

Shortly after Jacob was born, I reconnected briefly with my father. We had barely spoken over the years and my feelings toward him were not good. But I didn't want to deprive him of seeing his grandson, so I invited him over to the house. It was a strange situation having him over and seeing him with my son. But it was cool and it turned out to be a rare loving moment. I don't know if it really changed anything, but it was nice to see him.

Having Jacob helped Kristin and my relationship a little bit initially. But then I began to think about why we had gotten together in the first place. I had fallen in love with Kristin because I had been insecure about myself. I had asked her to marry me because I was afraid I was going to lose her. But I felt that she had trapped me by getting pregnant because she knew I wouldn't be going anywhere. Yeah, I know how shitty that sounds, but all I can say is that it was what I was thinking at the time.

The affair with Heather was still going strong. It wasn't until the second year of being together that she found out I was married. And she didn't care. It was weird. She just didn't care at all.

I felt guilty about the affair but clearly not guilty enough to end it. It was hard to be at home. It was hard to sleep in the same bed with Kristin. I was in love with my wife, but I was making love to both Kristin and Heather. It was easy to do, but it was hard to justify. I don't know if my behavior stemmed from the fact that my dad let my mom go out and be with men, but the fact remains that I made my own choices and I had to live with them. I figured there would be consequences for my actions, but I told myself I would just pay the consequences later. I really didn't feel any grief for what I was doing.

KRISTIN ORTIZ *At that point I had no idea he had a girlfriend. I knew something was up, but I tried to delude myself by saying, "Well, he's just traveling and he's busy." I was still thinking that we were going to live happily ever after. But he was a good liar.*

JOYCE ROBLES *Kristin told me one day that Tito had been cheating on her. It was heartbreaking, but there was nothing I could do. Eventually I did talk to Tito about it. I told him, "How can you do that to your wife and son?" His response was, "Well, it just happened." He didn't really want to talk to anybody about it, and he started pushing people away.*

It was at that point that I decided to see a psychiatrist for the first time. I felt it was a good idea to try to unload all the shit that was in my head. But after only a few sessions, the psychiatrist told me that there was so much stuff coming out of me that he didn't know how to deal with me. It was obvious that I needed some kind of help, but after those sessions I just put it aside and got back to business.

After the Matyushenko fight, I was considered unbeatable. Many people referred to me as the Ali of mixed martial arts. I got a real big head, and a lot of times, I was hard to be around.

That's when I decided to give acting a try. My first role was in a martial arts action movie called *Cradle 2 the Grave,* which starred the famous martial arts actor Jet Li. The reason I got into acting was because it looked easy and I wanted to try my hand at something else. As a fighter in the Octagon, I had always looked at myself as a kind of actor. I was making good money basically beating the shit out of myself. In *Cradle 2 the Grave* I played a cage fighter who fights another character who was played by Chuck Liddell.

There was not a whole lot of acting involved. Basically all we had to do was fight on cue. It was easy. When I wasn't working I would sit back and watch the other actors say their lines. I was surprised by how often they would mess up and how many chances they were given to deliver their lines perfectly.

After finishing the movie, it was time to defend my title again. This time it was the other Shamrock, Ken. Ken Shamrock is a real good fighter. I was not intimated by him, but I guess you could say I was a little bit afraid. I studied his fights closely. I thought if I could push him as hard as I possibly could during the match, he would quit.

Ken came to Ultimate Fighting after being in the WWE (World Wrestling Entertainment) and professional wrestling forever. He had been a great fighter for his time, but in the five years he had been away from mixed martial arts, our sport had evolved quite a bit in terms of style and training. I felt he was just out of step enough for me to take him.

It was time to start talking smack.

I told a lot of people in interviews that I was going to break Ken Shamrock's heart and his will. It was all part of the pre-fight hype, which was a game I was quite naturally good at playing.

And it worked, because on November 22, 2002, when I fought Ken Shamrock in UFC 40: Vendetta, we sold out the MGM Grand Ballroom, sixteen thousand seats, and had more than two hundred thousand pay-per-view buys in the United States alone. That fight was easily one of the biggest fights in UFC history.

And my father was there to watch it.

Inviting my father to come and watch me fight was a big move on my part. We had not spoken or seen each other since he had met Jacob. But I was at a stage in my life where I felt I should try to be a forgiving person and attempt to make peace with him.

So I got my father and his brother a pair of tickets. Now, when I'm in preparation for a fight I'm being steered in a lot of different directions and my mind is on a lot of things. I was getting ready to fight when I heard that my father had arrived in Vegas, but he couldn't remember which hotel was hosting the fight and he was lost. *Shit! What am I supposed to do?* I sent some guys out to look for him, and thankfully, they found him.

Limp Bizkit's "Break Stuff" brought me into the ring for the second fight in a row. I had slipped out of Nice Guy Tito Ortiz and into The Huntington Beach Bad Boy. It was fight time, and I was there to destroy Ken Shamrock.

I dominated that fight completely. I think he got maybe two punches in the whole fight. We fought for three rounds, and he didn't answer the bell for the fourth round. The ringside doctor had stepped in, looked at Shamrock, and said no more. I would later find out that I suffered a torn anterior cruciate ligament during the fight and would have to have surgery to fix it.

My victory T-shirt that night was probably one of my more humorous. I'm a big *South Park* fan. So I came up with a shirt that said: "I Just Killed Kenny! You Bastard!"

I don't know what happened to my father. Things always get crazy after a fight and I never met up with him. But at least he got to see me fight.

The victory over Ken Shamrock was a decisive one that pretty much clinched my reputation as an impossible-to-beat fighter. But you certainly couldn't tell by the way Dana White and the UFC were treating me.

After I fought Shamrock and I saw that the fees were going up and the pay-per-view was going through the roof,

I thought, *Okay, the UFC is making their money, it's time for me to make mine.* By this time the UFC had become a recognized, sanctioned sport. A lot of our fights were in Las Vegas, which added legitimacy to the organization. Ultimate Fighting was really taking off and was about ready to explode.

So I went to Dana again. His response was, "If it wasn't for me, you would be nothing!" After hearing that, I definitely felt like I was being taken for a ride. I was beginning to lose sleep and I came to the conclusion that Jim Gallow was not looking out for my best interests.

But the funny thing is that even when Dana became UFC president, I trusted him to do the right thing by me. The sad part was that I felt like I had given my life to him, and when I asked to be compensated for my efforts, things started getting worse.

The reality was that when I was out there asking for more money, I wasn't just asking for myself. I knew that if I got what I wanted, the UFC would have to pay the other fighters as well. I was doing the other fighters a favor, but I was doing it alone because everyone else was too intimidated. They thought they couldn't fight anywhere else because the UFC had pretty much bought up all the major regional fighting organizations. So they kept their mouths shut.

JOYCE ROBLES *Tito always said that his worst fear was being poor. But if he was having money or business problems, he kept it completely private from me.*

He would simply never let me know anything bad. If he had good news to share, I was one of the first people he told.

While the business side of my life was getting pretty shitty, my personal life was out of control as well.

I was still seeing Heather whenever I could, and once in a while, I was seeing other women too. Being with all those women was a physical thing, an ego boost and nothing else. And my guess was that the women I was with all wanted the same thing from me. They may have been after me for my money, but I really didn't know. I wasn't thinking much beyond just getting mine.

The only woman I really felt any kind of love for was Kristin, and she was the one I was cheating on. But as far as I could tell she didn't have a clue about Heather or anybody else. I was doing a damned good job of hiding it.

Until 2003.

CHAPTER TWELVE

Loss Times Two

*T*hat's when I started getting a little careless. Or maybe just a lot stupid.

I was on the phone with Heather one day and Kristin walked up the stairs. I immediately hung up. She wanted to know who I was talking to. I talked circles and got out of it.

I went out to make an appearance and called Heather on the drive home to tell her that I was going out later and that I would call her in a little while. I came home and jumped in the shower. While I was showering the phone rang. Heather had decided to call me back and when Kristin picked up the phone, Heather hung up.

By this time Kristin was starting to get a little suspicious. So she hit redial and ended up getting Heather's voice mail. Kristin left a message wanting to know who she was. A few minutes later Heather called back and told Kristin that she had been trying to get ahold of me to discuss a sponsorship deal. So thanks to Heather lying her ass off, I got away with it.

But I was starting to feel a bit uneasy about the close call and the relationship with Heather, so I steered clear of her for a couple of months. Then we got together again in Vegas, started hanging out, and, well, one thing led to another. While I was with Heather, Kristin called and asked me what I was doing in Vegas. I made an excuse about being there on UFC business, and then she asked if I was with anyone. Heather was right there in the room with me, but I said no.

But you know something? I think Kristin knew that something was going on. She always had this intuition. She had to know.

KRISTIN ORTIZ　*There reached a point when I knew he was having an affair. One night I had gone to bed early and had come downstairs for a glass of water. Tito was on the phone. As soon as he saw me, he hung up real quick. I asked him who he was talking to and he lied and told me it was a fighter friend. I said, "Oh really?" I grabbed the phone and called the guy. I asked if he had just talked to Tito and he said no. Tito broke down and said he was having an emotional affair with this girl. I was devastated. I didn't know what to do. So I kicked Tito out. He came back groveling and begging. He said he would end it and that he couldn't lose me or he would die. So I took him back. I really wanted to believe that he wasn't* *having a sexual relationship. We decided to try marriage counseling. But Tito was a very good liar. He had the marriage counselor convinced that I was paranoid. Finally I just brushed it under the rug and thought everything was going to be all right.*

What was going on with me at the time was not just limited to my affair with Heather. When you're the champion there are all kinds of temptations thrown in your path. And I have to admit that sometimes things got a little too crazy for me.

There was this time when I was passing through Alabama and this guy comes up to me and says that he wanted to give me his wife for the night. I said, "What the hell?" He said, "Yeah, I want you to fuck my wife." I said, "You've got to be out of your fucking mind." And yes, I did turn down his offer. That was just too weird for me. What was even weirder was that guys started offering me their wives and girlfriends all the time.

Fighters like me have never really had groupies the way rock stars do. I had a one-night stand with a ring card girl, and that was the closest thing to a groupie for me. Don't get me wrong, women were always coming on to me. Some of them thought I had money and they wanted to get their hands on it, and some . . . well, once in a while I would get drunk at a club and, you know, shit happened.

One thing that's interesting about mixed martial arts is

that men love us more than women do. Not in a homosexual way or anything—guys just love the fighting and the fighters. They'll come over, slap me on the back, and tell me what a badass I am. (For the record, I have no problem with gay people as long as they don't come on to me. And if they do, I just tell them that I don't swing that way.) But I've never had any really close friends among UFC fighters. I respect them, but I couldn't be their friend because that might, even on a subconscious level, impact how I fight them. About the time that things were starting to go downhill with Kristin, I learned a valuable lesson about being friendly with fighters.

The UFC wanted me to fight Chuck Liddell for my next title defense. I was all for it, but I knew that the UFC was making a shitload of money off the fights, and I wasn't about to agree to the fight for a measly $160,000. I wanted Chuck to band together with me and hold out for more money for the fight.

But Chuck folded. He said that all he cared about was winning the championship and that he would fight for whatever amount the UFC was offering. So the fight didn't happen because I sure as hell wasn't going to settle for less than what I thought I deserved. So instead Liddell fought Randy Couture for what the UFC would claim was a fight to determine the interim champion.

I was pissed off. I felt like I had been betrayed. I felt like everything I had worked so hard for had just been thrown out the window. The UFC had just taken my title away.

Couture beat Liddell and all of a sudden I was being

forced to fight Couture to maintain my title. Couture was forty-one years old at the time, and I had it in my heart that I was not going to lose to him. So I put my problems with the UFC and all the drama with Kristin and Heather out of my head, and made a conscious decision not to let any of it impact my performance.

Quite simply, I thought I was going to crush him. He was an older man. I really didn't respect him at all. I thought this was going to be an easy fight.

I went up to Big Bear and began training three months before the fight. Right in the middle of training I began to feel this extreme pain in my back. Doctors examined me and found that I had a bulging disk in my back. I was bedridden for four days and was given pills that would help with the inflammation of the disk. I did boxing, weight training, jujitsu, and running. But because of the disk I could not wrestle, and with somebody like Couture, you've got to wrestle.

The fight with Randy Couture took place September 25, 2003, and was billed as UFC 44: Undisputed. I was in as good shape as I could possibly be considering my back problems. But it wasn't good enough.

Couture dominated every round, and every round I dug a deeper hole for myself. I was trying to knock him out and he simply outwrestled me. He won in a five-round decision.

That was the first time I lost a fight in six years. To me it was like a loved one dying. It was tough trying to swallow that loss. To lose to Couture, well, it just hurt too much.

When I came home, Kristin could tell the difference. I certainly couldn't talk to Heather about it. I was hard on myself for two solid months. I cried all the time. I did a lot of drinking to kill my sorrows. I was very depressed. It was hard to lose a championship that I had held for four years. All of a sudden it seemed like everything was ripped out from under me.

Including my relationship with the UFC.

All of a sudden the UFC and, in particular, its president and my former manager, Dana White, didn't care about me anymore because now I wasn't the champion. They didn't like the fact that I was always asking for a bigger piece of the pay-per-view money and more money in general. I had a contract with the UFC that would end after the next three fights. And I was prepared to honor that contract.

Even though we were at odds, the UFC was smart enough to realize that I was still a major draw and they were quick to schedule another fight with me, the fight everybody had wanted to see. The fight with Chuck Liddell.

I was doing a lot of my training in the Los Angeles area and would only go up to Big Bear for the last six weeks. That was always my normal routine, but things were pretty intense between me and Kristin around the house, and being in Big Bear became a much-needed escape. Those kinds of distractions were the last thing I needed when I was preparing for a fight.

KRISTIN ORTIZ *Over the course of the next couple of years, things got worse. I was feeling real hatred for Tito. I just remember being fed up. I felt I either had to get out now before Jacob got older and got his heart broken or I had to stay in the relationship. I felt strongly that I didn't want Jacob to grow up thinking that it was okay to treat women the way Tito was treating me.*

It was like the last bit of love was slowly draining out of my marriage to Kristin. I continued to fool around. There really wasn't much left for us to say. We knew we both loved our son, and that was probably the only thing that was keeping us together.

But I think we both realized that Jacob was getting old enough to sense that his parents weren't happy, and that's no way for a kid to grow up. So I decided to try therapy for a second time. Seeing a psychiatrist while I was training for a fight was probably not the best idea. Being in therapy made me feel very soft. I would come out of the sessions feeling very weak and emotional—not the best way to feel when trying to build up a sufficient level of hostility for a fight.

Prior to the Liddell fight I received another acting offer in the film *The Crow: Wicked Prayer*. It was a step up from what I did in *Cradle 2 the Grave*. I played this real nasty character called Famine. I didn't think much of the script, but I learned a lot from the actors, especially Danny Trejo, who told me that as an actor I would spend more time waiting to act than actually acting. The film was not a huge success on any level, but it taught me a bit more about the craft, and acting was something I could see doing in the future.

The Liddell situation had not changed. He was still a good friend, but he didn't care about holding out for the money we deserved. I felt like he had sold out, but he was going to fight to be the best, and I couldn't look down on him for that. After all, you have to fight the best to be the best.

The fight with Chuck was simply billed as UFC 47: It's On and was held on May 2, 2004. He was dominating me in the first round. I was kind of holding my own, but I couldn't take him down. In the second round, he went to throw a punch just as I was throwing a punch and his thumb got me in the eye. I stepped back, wiped my eye, and couldn't see a thing. I managed to block about six shots and then the next four connected and he dropped me. The referee stepped in and stopped it.

I lost.

In the meantime my relationship with Kristin was just about shot. She had chosen to ignore my affairs for a while, but I wasn't making any attempts to hide Heather from her anymore.

On one occasion I went to Calgary, Canada, with a friend of mine named Damian. I probably told Kristin that it was business related, but I was really just looking for an excuse to get out of town and party a little bit. Damian and I went to a strip club and brought some chicks back to our room. When I got home, Kristin was going through my bags and she found a condom. I told her it wasn't mine. I told her that I had put all my clothes in a drawer and that Damian must have dropped it in there. She didn't believe me for a second.

The arguments became more and more intense between us until the relationship finally came to an end.

Kristin smokes, and I just hate people who smoke. She quit when she got pregnant, but when Jacob was born she started smoking again. One day, I had just gotten home from training and I had my foot in an ice bucket. We were arguing back and forth, and one of the things we were arguing about was her smoking. At one point I said, "Well, at least Heather doesn't fucking smoke!" Kristin wound up and hit me real hard across the face.

I looked up at her and thought, *I should punch this bitch in her fucking face.*

But I've never hit a woman in my life. Instead I took my foot out of the ice bucket and tossed the water on her. She was soaked from head to toe. I got up, said I was done, and walked out.

KRISTIN ORTIZ *I remember the day it was finally over. We started screaming at each other. All I could think of at that point was,* He doesn't like us, he doesn't want to be here. *That's when I hit him in the face and he threw the water at me. Then he left.*

To be honest, I was relieved, and my guess was that Kristin was, too. Our relationship hadn't been working for a long time. She would always be a part of my life, personally and professionally. She was good at handling my business, and I wasn't going to be one of those guys who splits with his woman and leaves her with nothing. Kristin would always be taken care of.

KRISTIN ORTIZ *A week after Tito walked out, we sat down and talked. We realized that we had to separate. He insisted that he would cover things financially and take care of all the bills. Later on I would realize that this was his way of taking care of the guilt he was feeling about the end of the relationship.*

JOYCE ROBLES *It broke my heart when Kristin and Tito broke up. I thought they were going to be together forever.*

We were not separated at that point, but we were essentially living two separate lives. And I no longer had to make any pretense about cheating.

For the next year and a half I would date a lot of different chicks. I began to pull away from Heather. I know for a fact that she was with other guys when I wasn't with her. When we were together it was only about the sex. I never for a moment saw any kind of real future with Heather.

I went through a lot of shit over the next few months. Even though Kristin and I had for all intents and purposes split up, we were still arguing. Right in the middle of all that, the UFC called to tell me they wanted me to fight Patrick Côté.

This was Côté's first UFC fight, and with all the experience I had it seemed like a pretty easy fight. But with all the personal distractions in my life and the fact that I had suffered back-to-back losses, I actually had more to lose, so this fight was a bit of a risk.

There were just too many distractions in Los Angeles and I really didn't feel like going up to Big Bear, so I packed all my stuff and moved to Las Vegas to train. While I was in Vegas, I decided to switch trainers. My longtime trainer wasn't too happy with my decision, but I hooked up with another trainer, Master Toddy, and we worked well together.

Côté definitely put up a tougher fight than I expected. In the first round he hit me with a solid right that knocked me to my knees. Trading punches with him was going to be tougher than I thought. I stepped up the elbow and forearm smashes. It was more of the same in the second round—a lot of punches. By the third round I was definitely trying to ground and pound rather than beat him with a submission. But he hung in there.

It was a real tough fight. I had to hand it to Côté—he put up quite a battle. But I felt I had beaten him. I ended up winning a unanimous decision against him. It was not my best fight, but it was a win. I celebrated for a while like I usually did after a fight, but then there were some realities I had to deal with.

Now, all of a sudden, I had no trainer, my personal life was a mess, and I was right in the middle of trying to renegotiate a new contract with the UFC without a manager.

Life had been better.

CHAPTER THIRTEEN

Crash and Burn

*T*he last fight on my contract with the UFC was coming up soon. They were after me to re-sign and I refused.

I was not about to renegotiate at that time, because they were offering me shit—worse than my previous contract. They knew as well as I did that if I won the last fight on my contract, I would be holding all the cards. They also knew how important I was to the growth of the UFC.

I had been a champion for four years, and the UFC pushed me out in front and used me as the poster boy for the organization. I had the right image, the charisma, all the things they wanted to see in one of their fighters. I was articulate. I spoke my mind. I did promotion. I did charity work. I was the star they wanted to help push their sport. And now they were giving me shit.

After the Côté fight, I was on my own. I had no trainer. I had pretty much had it with my management. Kristin and I were barely speaking. So I moved to Huntington Beach and got an apartment with a friend of mine. And then the UFC announced that my last fight on my current contract would be with Vitor Belfort.

Belfort was a good fighter. He was a former lightweight champion. And as it always seemed to be, I needed the money from this fight very badly. My contract at the time indicated that I would get fifty percent of my purse if I showed up and fifty percent if I won the match. So if I lost the Belfort fight, I stood to lose eighty grand.

Needless to say, I was not going to lose that fight.

The only problem was that three months before the fight I had not done any training and still didn't have a trainer. At the suggestion of one of my friends, I called up a trainer named Saul Soliz and asked him if he would step in and train me. He said he would love to do it.

We went up to Big Bear about six weeks before the fight. Big Bear was a miserable place to train at that time of year. There was a major snowfall, and everything was frozen. We had to drive all over the place just to find a place for me to run. It was hell.

But by the end of those six weeks I felt I was ready for Belfort.

The fight was held on February 6, 2005. It was called UFC 51: Super Saturday. I had come into the arena carrying both the American and Mexican flags to honor my mixed-race heritage. The crowd was going crazy. My recent losses had clearly not diminished my support among the fans.

All I can say is that Belfort and I had a real good scramble.

I started the match by taking him down. Then we went back and forth for a long time. At one point he hit me with a left hook and broke my nose. I scrambled out and took him down. I was on top of him and there was blood streaming out of my nose and all over him.

I was thinking, *Holy shit! I'd better keep hitting him before the referee stops this thing.* So I kept punching him and then the round was finally over. In the corner after the first round my cut man was working on me, wiping the blood off and checking on the break. He said it wasn't that bad. I went out and dominated the second round. In the third round I finally gassed him out. He had nothing left, and I ended up winning a three-round split decision.

After the fight ended I put on my now customary victory shirt. But this one was different. Rather than saying something derogatory about the fighter I had just beaten, it read: "Bring Home Our Troops!" Then I picked up the flags I had come into the arena with and ran to the top of the balcony, waving the flags over my head as the crowd went nuts.

I don't remember making a conscious effort to begin to clean up my image. I'd like to think that what I did that night was just my way of supporting the troops. But however people took it, they sure noticed.

I was on top, and everything was in my hands now. Unfortunately the UFC did not get the message.

After that fight, we got down to some serious contract negotiations. I felt that I could negotiate my own contract, so I went in without anybody representing me. I really didn't need any help because I knew exactly what I wanted. But as it turned out, the UFC and Dana White were very mean and disrespectful toward me.

They took me off the UFC website completely. They blurred out anything on the website or advertisements that mentioned Punishment. I was taken out of all their commercials. It seemed as if their answer to my asking for a fair contract was to pretty much wipe me out of UFC history. Then things got really nasty.

Dana turned into a complete and utter asshole.

He would say in interviews, "I made Tito Ortiz and I'll make him forgotten." The whole situation seemed to go from bad to worse. Dana was playing hardball, but Lorenzo Fertitta made it clear that the UFC did not want to lose me. And so the negotiations dragged on, not really getting anywhere.

And I was faced with fighting a billion-dollar company.

Word had traveled fast that my contract with the UFC was up, and I began getting offers from competing organizations. Pride out of Japan made an offer for a six-fight deal, but it was essentially the same money I was being offered by the UFC. Besides, the competition was a lot stiffer with Pride and there was a good chance that I would be fighting out of my weight division, so I turned it down.

The WFA (Wrestling Federation of America) was offering me what I wanted. But if I was going to basically help build the company from the ground up, I wanted a piece of the company, which they were not willing to give me.

Finally I decided that it was time to take the biggest chance of my career—I forced the UFC's hand. I said, "Okay, I'll sit out and we'll see how you guys do without me."

My walking away from the UFC was big news. The press was all over it. The fans seemed to like the idea of my going up against the UFC, and that made me feel kind of good.

But I was smart enough to realize that if I sat out and did absolutely nothing, people would begin to forget about me. That happened a lot to fighters—once they stopped fighting, they were forgotten. That wasn't going to happen to me. I hired a publicist and began to do other things to keep my name out there.

For the next year I was not involved in mixed martial arts with the UFC or any other fighting organization. But that did not mean I wasn't busy. I did some talk shows and some other things for the publicity. I did a series of fighting technique seminars that were pretty much paying the bills at that point.

In May 2005, I sort of got back into the fighting game when I signed an agreement to appear with Total Non-stop Action Wrestling. But not as a fighter—at least, not directly.

On May 15, 2005, under the name Hard Justice Ortiz, I served as a special guest referee in the NWA (National Wrestling Alliance) World Heavyweight Championship between Jeff Jarrett and A. J. Styles. At one point in the match, Jarrett shoved me and I knocked him out, which allowed Styles to win the fight. I refereed a second match in October.

I had a chance to experience that whole side of professional wrestling as entertainment. It was fun and it kept me in front of the camera, which was the important thing . . . because nobody was telling me that they wanted me to fight again.

One night I had been watching a UFC event on TV and was feeling left out. All of a sudden, it was like I didn't exist. I was feeling pretty sorry for myself. I already had too much to drink, but now I was ready to go out and party. I shouldn't have been drinking and driving, but I had crazy thoughts in my head—I guess you could call them suicidal.

I was thinking about how cool it would be if I just crashed.

I hit the center divider. My car was launched into space and tore into a light pole on the other side of the street. The light pole went down, but the car kept going. It hit a wall and then it slid into a pine tree. The impact of the crash compressed the entire car on my legs. Luckily I had friends following behind me in another car, and they called for help.

There were chunks of my car everywhere, and blood was pumping out of me. The ambulance and the fire department showed up. It took forty-five minutes using the Jaws of Life to pry me out of the car. They took me to the hospital. Fortunately, it all looked a lot worse than it turned out to be.

I had some cuts and bruises, but I guess I just got lucky. I didn't realize how lucky until later in the evening when I went back out to the wreckage to get some of my belongings out of the car. The tow truck driver was there. He said, "You don't know how lucky you are. Most of the time when I come to an accident this bad, the driver is usually dead."

When the tow truck driver told me that, I was stunned. I looked upon that accident as a sign.

I knew I had reached a point where I was being very careless with my life and that I really didn't give a shit anymore.

A friend of mine drove me back to my home. Kristin was at the door when I showed up and she said, "Oh shit, you were fighting!" I told her that I totaled my car and almost died. Then I broke down and started crying uncontrollably. A lot of shit in my life came pouring out of me. That night Kristin and I talked about a lot of stuff. We both knew that our relationship had been over for a long time. Kristin wasn't happy. I sure as hell wasn't happy. I was an emotional wreck. All the guilt and sneaking around and lying had ground me down.

Kristin deserved a whole lot more than what I was giving her, and that became crystal clear the more we talked. I only had one thing to say to Kristin that made any sense.

I told her I wanted to start my life all over again.

KRISTIN ORTIZ *After a year apart I realized that Tito still loved Jacob and me in the best way he knows how. I knew he would die for us. All of a sudden we became friends again. I was past the hurt.*

CHAPTER FOURTEEN

Back from the Dead

*I*n the summer of 2005, Dana White said in an interview that as long as he was president, Tito Ortiz would never fight in the UFC again. But apparently there were other people interested in me.

My manager, pretty much in name only, stepped in and was going back and forth with the UFC. I was not surprised that Jim Gallow's negotiations with Dana were not going anywhere. I might as well have been negotiating myself, which, in a sense, I was.

In the meantime, the WFA still wanted to sign me. But then it turned out that the UFC was negotiating an *Ultimate Fighter* series with Spike TV, and a lot of people were telling the executives at Spike TV that they ought to be signing me because I would be great on television.

Word got back to Dana White and the UFC and it put a lot of pressure on them. I'm not going to lie to you and say

I wasn't having a good time watching Dana and the UFC squirm. They wanted me signed, and it really seemed like they were losing the public relations war. At that point, I was seriously thinking about signing with the WFA and screwing Dana White and the UFC.

Sure, I wanted more money, but the big thing I was pushing for on my new contract was the very thing I had to give up on my last contract, which was owning my own image. I wanted a piece of whatever they were making off my name and likeness.

The whole time I had been away, support from fans and people whose opinion meant something to the UFC had been growing. They finally looked at the bottom line and at the number of people who supported me and realized that they couldn't let me go.

Especially to a competing organization.

So they grudgingly signed me to a three-fight deal. I got an extra $50,000 per fight and a bigger piece of the pay-per-view income. I got a percentage of my own image and I was given the *Ultimate Fighter* series season-three coaching position. I had finally gotten my way on the two most important deal points of the contract—more money and the rights to my likeness. Negotiating for a role in the *Ultimate Fighter* show was gravy, and I saw it as a great way to get the word out on the sport. The first two seasons had done real well and with the backing of Spike TV, it was a given that the third season would be a smash—and I wanted in.

So part of my new deal was to be one of the *Ultimate*

Fighter trainers. I asked Dana if we could get Ken Shamrock to be the other trainer. I thought Shamrock would be good on a competitive level, and I felt that he and I should fight at the conclusion of the season. It would be a good build for the show because I knew Ken was a good fighter and that he could talk smack.

Ken and I met before the beginning of the season. It was a bit tense. We had never really gotten along and we had talked a lot of smack. So putting us together in this type of situation could be asking for trouble. But I went up to him at the beginning of the season and said, "You know, we're here for a job and to see who's the best coach. I'm going to respect your space as long as you respect mine." He agreed. During the entire run of the show, I never said anything to him or so much as looked at him wrong.

We shot thirteen episodes in six weeks. A lot of people thought I was acting and playing to the camera, but that wasn't the case at all. I just used my skills as a coach and a trainer. Every guy who I picked for my team was a guy that I wanted. I don't think a lot of guys wanted to be on Shamrock's team; they clearly wanted to be on mine. Once we started training, I was beginning to think that Shamrock didn't really know what he was doing. I put my guys through all-around testing, while Ken just tested to see who was the strongest guy.

Once the actual matches began, I started talking a little bit of smack. My team ended up winning nine of the twelve matches and after each win I would turn to him and say, "How does that feel? You must be doing something wrong." I know that got under his skin. The big issue during the filming of the series was that they wanted me to talk more shit to Shamrock, but I wouldn't. For me this was a great learning experience, and talking a lot of smack was not what this was about.

The *Ultimate Fighter* series did a lot for me. People were used to seeing the Bad Boy in the Octagon. They hadn't had a chance to see me as a coach and more of a person.

My first fight after completing the *Ultimate Fighter* series was to be against a previous *Ultimate Fighter* series winner, Forrest Griffin. Griffin was a solid fighter and a good guy. He was aggressive and had nothing to lose. I had everything to lose, so I knew this was going to be a tough first fight. I knew he would come out swinging for the fences.

I went up to Big Bear to train. But the truth was, I knew I shouldn't have been fighting.

I was having a lot of physical problems. I still had issues with that bulging disk in my back and a torn ACL, I still had some problems from the back injuries from when I fought Couture, and I also had a knee that was giving me problems.

There was the usual pre-fight hype and a bit of trash talking. A lot of people did not see this as a very competitive fight, and Dana White was doing his best to drum up interest, saying things like "Forrest Griffin is a better fighter than Tito Ortiz ever was" and stuff like that. But I didn't hold anything personal against Forrest. I was convinced that I was going to go out and beat his ass.

I wasn't a hundred percent. I was only training a couple of days a week and I was in no shape at all. But I did spend a lot of time thinking about what the T-shirt for this fight should say. I finally realized that this wasn't about Forrest or the fight; this was about me. Finally I came up with something.

The fight with Forrest Griffin was called UFC 59: Reality Check. Because of physical problems, the fight was close. In the first round, I just dominated. I took him down and punished the shit out of him. But I blew my wad in the first round and so, in the second round, I was a little tired. In the third round I was totally gassed until the last minute and a half. Then I got a takedown and won the round and the match.

I put on the shirt. A lot of people were expecting a put-down of Forrest. But what they got instead was: "With Great Sacrifice Comes Great Rewards." It was a T-shirt for me, and I felt that I deserved it.

My second fight with Ken Shamrock was being billed as a grudge match of sorts. I don't know why. I was always talking smack about the guy, but I did not really hate him or anything. I guess it was just the normal buildup to a fight in order to put people in the seats.

I fought Shamrock on July 8, 2006. It was billed as UFC 61: Bitter Rivals. It really wasn't much of a fight unless you were rooting for me.

I got him down and elbowed him in the face a bunch of times, and the referee stopped it at 1:23 of the first round. Shamrock complained about the stoppage after the fight. All I could say was, "Just look at the tape of the fight." The tape showed that he had been knocked unconscious.

My T-shirt that night was quite simply a statement of fact: "If You Fight Tito Ortiz You Lose!"

But he still continued to complain about how he had been robbed. I told him, "If you didn't think I kicked your ass, we can do it again." The third fight between us, Ortiz vs Shamrock 3: The Final Chapter, was held on September 10, 2006. It was on Spike TV, and we had something like ten million viewers.

There was the usual hype and trash talking. I liked Ken Shamrock even less now. A lot of what passes for trash talking is pretty humorous sometimes, but I can honestly say that by the time we got around to that third fight, I was really pissed off at him.

Ken came out and tried to take me down. I muscled him into the cage. He tried for my leg and missed. That's when I got him up against the cage and just started punching him. I stopped him at 2:45 of the first round. And yes, I knocked him unconscious.

Shamrock and I have had our words over the years, and to this day we're not the best of friends. But we embraced after that fight and I think, to a degree, we buried the hatchet.

Although I did manage to get in one final shot with

the T-shirt I wore that night: "Punishing Him Into Retirement."

The third fight with Shamrock marked the end of my current contract with the UFC. By then I did not have management or an attorney. Dana was being all nice to me now and he reminded me that I was making good money. I had to agree.

I was back on the hot seat again.

I told Dana, "Look, I'm going to trust you completely. Give me the contract and I'll sign it and send it back to you." It must have killed Dana to give me the contract that he did. He gave me a $200,000 signing bonus and raised my fee to a full million dollars a fight.

Given my relationship with Dana and the bad blood that was growing between us, a lot of people thought I was crazy to take his offer. It was kind of a ballsy move. But I knew that at the end of the day, business is business and that Dana White and the UFC had a lot to lose if they screwed me over on this contract.

I signed the agreement and was back in business with the UFC.

CHAPTER FIFTEEN

Jenna

*A*s much as I craved the spotlight, by 2005 I was so recognizable that occasionally it was annoying. I couldn't go to dinner without someone bothering me. I couldn't go to the mall or do anything without someone coming up to me for an autograph or to take a picture. But hell, I really didn't have too much to complain about. I had been dying for this kind of attention my whole life, so I guess this is just the price you pay for celebrity. Every once in a while I wish I could put on a mask or be someone else for a day. But I'm a big guy, so it's kind of hard for me to hide.

And then I met Jenna Jameson in June 2006.

The first time I saw one of Jenna's movies was when I was working at Spanky's. My reaction to her at that time was like any guy watching porn—I was just thinking like a guy with his other head.

When I was nineteen years old, I was doing some work

for a company out in Vegas that was setting up booths for a convention. It turned out one of the booths was for Jenna. I saw her from far away and didn't go up to her. But boy, I could tell she was hot.

JENNA JAMESON *Tito told me years later that he saw me there but he didn't have the guts to come up to me. He said that we shook hands, but I don't really remember. If we did, I wish he would have said something.*

The third time I met Jenna went like this. I had been up in Big Bear, training for the second Ken Shamrock fight, when I decided to take a day off and come down to Los Angeles to watch a hockey game. My friend Chris Nagy and I were in one of the suites, watching the game, and there were several girls in there with us. We started talking to them and I mentioned that I had to go to Vegas to do some public relations for the upcoming Shamrock fight. The girls said they would be in Vegas, too, and that their friend Jenna was going as well.

"You know," said the girl. "Jenna Jameson?"

I knew exactly who Jenna Jameson was.

One girl said, "Yeah, maybe you can come out and party with us. Jenna and her husband aren't getting along and they may be divorcing soon."

This was getting interesting.

JENNA JAMESON *I had been a fan of the UFC for a long time* *and had been to a lot of Tito's matches. Tito was always so outspoken, but I saw something in him other than being crazy and a loudmouth. I never really thought about approaching him because, at the time, I was either married or had a boyfriend. I remember being at the Hard Rock in Vegas one time and he walked by and we locked eyes for a moment. But I didn't go up to him because he was so goddamned intimidating. At that point, I really would not have known what to say to him.*

After meeting the girls, I went back up to Big Bear and a couple of days later I was checking the friend requests on my MySpace page when I saw one from Jenna Jameson. I thought it was a joke. So I e-mailed her back and said, "This isn't Jenna Jameson, you're lying. E-mail me back if it's really you."

JENNA JAMESON *So I emailed him back and said, "Here's my phone number. Call me and I'll prove that I'm Jenna."*

I went out to train and when I came back there was an e-mail saying, "Yes, this is Jenna. I've been watching your fights for a long time. I'm going to be in Vegas to watch your match and I'd like to come to your after party." I called and told her my after party was going to be at the club Tryst and that she should come by.

The next week I went up to Vegas for the pre-fight promotion and I saw her there with her husband. She came over and introduced herself. Man, she was hot! I was acting rather shy because that's how I usually am when I meet a woman for the first time. She turned to her husband and said, "He's hot!" To which he said, "Yeah, he's your fucking type!" That's when they were fighting. We made some conversation and then I went off to prepare for the fight with Shamrock, which was held at the Mandalay Bay.

After the fight I went to the Tryst club. I looked around and there she was. I had started drinking early and was already pretty drunk. Her security guard came over to me and told me she wanted to talk to me. I was a little nervous so I asked a couple of friends to come over with me.

JENNA JAMESON *When I showed up and had my security people go over to him, he was shocked. He was scared shitless, and I could tell that he was really shy to talk to me. So I started talking to him.*

I sat down next to her. I was pretty fucked up, but I tried to play it cool. She told me that she saw my fight and wanted to come out and talk to me. We made some small talk for a while.

JENNA JAMESON *Tito sat down. He was so shy that he couldn't even look at me. I remember kind of scaring him when I told him I was single. He looked at me and started laughing because he was so*

*embarrassed that he really didn't know what to
say. You could tell he wanted to ask me out but
he didn't have the guts.*

Then she said, "What are you doing tomorrow? I'll be going to the Hard Rock." I said, "Cool! I'm actually staying there. So I guess I'll see you there."

We exchanged cell phone numbers and I actually saw her again the next night. That was an interesting encounter.

I was still seeing Heather when I was in town, and she was with me that night. But we were not dating anymore. I spotted Jenna across the room and pointed her out to Heather, who looked pissed. She said, "So who gives a fuck! Fuck her!"

Heather was jealous. That was good. She was never a real serious thing to me. She was even less so now. When I was in Vegas we would just get together and have sex. I didn't want a girlfriend. But I started seeing Jenna.

JENNA JAMESON *A few days after I met Tito for the first time, I met up with him at the Hard Rock. I walked in and was taken to his table. Tito wobbled over and he was a little bit messed up. He sat down next to me and all of a sudden it was a different Tito than the guy I had met a couple of nights before. Suddenly he was a lot more forward. He put his arm around me and started whispering all this crazy shit in my ear. Stuff like, "I've*

*watched your movies. I'm a huge fan. I know
everything about you and we should date." He
was coming on to me so strong and throwing me
so much game that I was actually taken aback.
I remember texting my friend at one point in
the evening and telling him that Tito was really
a jackass.*

One night I was with Jenna and Heather walked up behind her and stuck her finger in her butt. Jenna says, "What the fuck!" and yells at her security to get "that fucking chick" out of here.

JENNA JAMESON *Suddenly this girl walks by and puts her finger
down my butt crack. I have a real problem
with people touching me when I don't want to
be touched. I turned around and gave her the
Jameson glare. The girl says, "Oh, she's so fine. I
would fuck her." Then my security guy grabbed
her.*

The security guy seemed kind of flustered. He told Jenna that the girl was actually my girlfriend, but I made it clear to her that although she was with me, she wasn't my chick.

JENNA JAMESON *I had no idea Tito was dating anybody. Obviously,
he didn't tell me. I got up and got out of there.
Tito hadn't made a real good impression on me,*

and that business with his supposed girlfriend didn't help matters. But Tito kept texting me over the next few days, saying that he wasn't dating Heather.

The next day I told Heather that I was going to go out on a date with Jenna. Heather said, "Well, in that case, I'm never going to talk to you again."

My response to that was, "Oh well. I don't give a fuck."

A week went by. I'd had my son with me for four days and he was getting ready to go home with Kristin. Things between us had gotten much better once we were separated. We were actually starting to be more like the friends we were when we first met.

After Jacob went home, I gave Jenna a call and asked her if she wanted to go to the county fair with me.

"You're asking me to the fair?" she asked.

I said, "Yeah, it's cool."

"That's so cute," she replied. "But I can't go. I've got things to do."

JENNA JAMESON *Tito asking me to the fair got me hook, line, and sinker. I thought,* Oh my God! This guy is so sweet! *Instead of coming out with a line like, "Oh, I'll take you shopping in my Rolls-Royce," he was asking me out to the county fair.*

She told me that she and some of her friends were going out in LA on Friday and that I was welcome to come along.

At that point I was still a little shy around Jenna so I called my friend Rick and invited him to come with me.

JENNA JAMESON *Tito walked into my room. There were a lot of people there and it had turned into some kind of party. Tito went off to the bar we had set up and sat there by himself. He was so shy. And based on what I had seen of him at the Hard Rock, I realized that alcohol was not a good mix for him. I was like,* Look at this guy. He's this big guy who crushes people for a living and he's sitting over there like a seventeen-year-old boy.

We met Jenna and her friends at the hotel Mondrian in Hollywood. I was sitting on a couch with her all evening and I kept moving closer and closer, until finally I put my arm around her.

We were having a great conversation. I couldn't believe how smart she was. That was easily the best conversation I had ever had with a woman in my life. We started walking out at the end of the evening and she was kind of walking by herself, so I grabbed her arm and pulled her close to me.

We were pretty much together after that.

JENNA JAMESON *At one point during the evening we decided we were going to go clubbing. Tito kind of positioned himself next to me as we left the room.*

I thought that was cute and that it took some balls. As we were walking, he grabbed my hand. I was thinking, Oh my god! How cute is this? *All that night he was so attentive; you could tell that he was really into me. At that point I was thinking I could fall in love with this guy.*

Around the time Tito and I started dating, I was seen out and photographed with Dave Navarro. I really wanted to keep my personal life under wraps at that time. And Dave and I were really good friends, so he was willing to be seen in public and to give the impression that we were dating. The reason I went to such lengths to keep my relationship with Tito a secret was that I knew something was going to come of it and I didn't want the press and paparazzi to get wind of it yet. I don't believe Tito was aware of what I was doing at that point. Because the reality was that I was with Tito every second of the day and it was all about us. But eventually somebody photographed us and, boom, it hit the press and there was nothing I could do about it.

We didn't have sex for about a month. But it was worth the wait. As I was getting to know her, I found her to be a very respectable girl. Which was not the impression I had of women who worked in porn.

After working at Spanky's and being around that business, I had the impression that a porno chick is easy—you go and fuck her and it's no big thing. But I got a totally different vibe from Jenna. I respect her a whole lot.

JENNA JAMESON *Early on in the relationship I discovered that Tito really valued me as a person. What we had went beyond just a physical relationship. It was a friendship. Once Tito and I started getting serious, we didn't even have to say we were getting serious. We just knew it was happening.*

I did have second thoughts about getting involved with Jenna. I obviously knew all about her background, so I had to ask myself what I was getting into. She explained to me that she had gotten out of the business a while ago and that the only sexual activity she had in the past three years had been with her husband. I truly believe she is done with porn. She's a former porno star. If she were still in the business, I might not still be with her after more than a year.

And no, I never cheated on her with other women. There has been no fooling around since we got together. Zero cheating. It used to eat me up when I cheated on Kristin. It hurt so bad that I couldn't look myself in the mirror. With Jenna I don't have the urge to cheat. All of that has changed for me.

She's beautiful. She has an awesome body. She's smart. We care about each other. She's not with me for my money. The fact is she has more money than I do. We're kind of like a celebrity power couple and we empower each other.

KRISTIN ORTIZ *I was kind of relieved when I found out he was involved with Jenna. He was finally involved with somebody who wasn't out for his money. She wasn't a stripper who was trying to get knocked up and get her hands on his money.*

JENNA JAMESON *Tito said he really wanted me to meet Kristin. I thought,* Oh God! People automatically think I'm a monster because I'm a porn star. I don't know if this is such a good idea. *If I didn't get along with Kristin, the mother of Tito's child, the relationship between us would never work. But Tito told me that he had talked to Kristin about me, that we would get along really well, and that he wanted me to meet her. I didn't really know if I wanted this to happen, and I guess I would have to say Tito kind of shoved it on me.*

KRISTIN ORTIZ *I had flown to California to meet with Tito on some business matters. I was on my way over to his house when he called and asked me if I was ready to meet Jenna. When he told me she was over there now, I said, "I guess I'm going to have to be."*

JENNA JAMESON *It was kind of an awkward moment. I came down the stairs and she was sitting on the couch. I think it was more awkward for Kristin than it* *was for me. I think she felt that we all had to be friends no matter what because Tito loved me, he loved Kristin, and he loved his son. It was a quick hello, I shook her hand and then left. It was just an uncomfortable moment all around. But the relationship would grow and we would become good friends.*

I was kind of scared about how it was all going to turn out. I had told Kristin that I was in love with Jenna and that she makes me happy. Kristin was fine with that. To be honest, she was happy that I was finally with a woman who was not after my money.

And there had been quite a few of those. I didn't always have the best judgment when it came to women. I was out for having sex with a lot of different women and I didn't think too far beyond that.

Jenna was a little uncomfortable at first. She had never dated anybody who had a kid with somebody else. So yeah, it was hard for her. But over time they've gotten to know each other and it's become a more comfortable situation for both of them.

KRISTIN ORTIZ *I think initially she had a harder time dealing with me than I did with her. She was in a new relationship and she had to get used to the fact that Tito had a kid with somebody else and that we were still good friends and business partners.*

JOYCE ROBLES *When Tito told me about Jenna, I had no idea who she was. When I found out about her background, it didn't bother me at all. When I met her, it was easy to see why Tito was crazy about her.*

KRISTIN ORTIZ *About a year after Tito and I separated, Tito's friend Wayne told me something that made so much sense. He said Tito had always dreamed of living a normal life with the white picket fence, the wife, the kid, and the dog. With Jacob and me, he had the American dream. But the problem was that when he was in it, he couldn't stand it. I guess, given how he grew up, it was way too normal for him. He'll always want it, but he can't stand living it. His idea of normal is being in the spotlight and traveling and going to parties. With Jenna he has a partner who is into doing those things.*

I'm not going to lie to you and say that being with Jenna has been one easy ride. We're great when we're alone together. It's how the rest of the world has reacted that has made for some interesting situations—one of which put me in direct conflict with the U. S. Marines.

I have been a supporter of our troops for a long time and became a favorite with the Marines. I was always going down to Camp Pendleton to talk to the guys, and I guess they looked up to me as this fighter and entertainer. One day I got an invite from a lieutenant in the Marine Corps Air Station in Miramar, California, to come to their annual Birthday Ball and to be one of their honorees. The guy on the phone said all I had to do was come down and speak in front of a couple of thousand people.

I said, "Awesome, I would love to do that." He told me I could bring a guest and I let him know that I'd be bringing my girlfriend, Jenna. There was an uneasy pause at the other end of the line.

"You don't mean your girlfriend, Jenna Jameson?"

I said yes and he told me that I couldn't bring her. I asked why, and the lieutenant stammered and said that it was a decision by the marine higher-ups that I would not be allowed to bring her.

I said, "That's bullshit! She's not even in the business anymore!"

His response was that she still had something to do with that industry. I got real mad at that point. "She's living the American Dream," I said, "and you don't give a shit about that? Who doesn't watch porn? Are you guys embarrassed that one of your guys may have seen her in a porno movie before?" We went back and forth on this for a while.

Finally, I told him I couldn't go to the event. I explained that I'm in love with this girl and I respect her one hundred percent. How could I tell her that I was not going to take her to the Marines' Ball because the Marines didn't want to accept her? I didn't go.

JENNA JAMESON *Tito refusing to go without me said a lot about his character. He wanted me there with him because I was a part of his life. I think what the Marines said to Tito really shocked him. I sat down with him after he refused to go and told him I didn't want him to feel that he had to fight for my honor. But he said that he loved me and that he would always fight for my honor. That really touched me.*

The Marines realized they screwed up and tried to save face after the fact. First they tried to turn the whole thing around, saying how could they allow an Ultimate Fighter to bring his porn star girlfriend to a Marine ball. That didn't go over so well. Then they apologized and said it wasn't up to them and that some higher-ups had made the decision. And then they actually invited Jenna to come down to various events for the troops.

But Jenna being treated that way was a hard thing to deal with. I still support the troops and I'm convinced that if we had gone, they would have accepted Jenna for who she is.

But I won't let anybody disrespect my woman. Not even the Marines.

Which leads me to a situation that happened in 2006 that involved Jenna and how I came close to having to hurt somebody—somebody whose name you will no doubt recognize.

Jenna and I and a couple of my friends were at Hugh

Hefner's Playboy Mansion for this big party. There were a lot
of famous people there. One of them, the rapper Too Short,
had just finished performing and it was obvious that he was
drunk.

After his show, he was walking around and he walked up
to where Jenna and I and my friend Damian were standing.
He starts rapping to her, saying stuff like, "Hey sweet thing.
How you doing?" I got up in his face and said, "Yeah, dawg,
that's my lady." But then he kept right on rapping to her.

JENNA JAMESON *That was a total nightmare. I just covered my
eyes and thought,* Okay, the reign of terror is
about to begin. *I expected punches to be thrown
right away. I turned away, which has always
been the signal for Tito to handle it.*

I thought, *I can't believe this motherfucker is doing this
right now, disrespecting Jenna and me right in front of my face.* I
was getting real pissed. I thought, *That's Too Short, but I don't
give a fuck because that's my lady.* So I got in his face again
and said, "Excuse me, but that's my girl." He just said, "Hey,
chill, man, chill," and he started rapping to her again. Now
I was getting really angry.

I turned to my friend Damian and said, "You'd better
stop this fucking shit or I'm going to stomp a fucking hole
in his face!" Jenna heard all this going down and kept saying,
"Stop! Stop! Stop!"

But it was too late.

Damian, who is a pretty big guy, went over to Too Short

and told him, "You'd better walk away right now or you're going to get a hole stomped in your face." Too Short said "What?" Damian turned to me and said, "Tito, I'll slap his ass for you." I didn't want to get kicked out of the Playboy Mansion and not be able to come back, so I cooled down.

But I think Too Short got the message because he turned around and walked away. But my thing with Too Short wasn't over.

Two weeks later I was in Vegas, taking part in a UFC event. I was taking a picture with a fan and Too Short walked right by me and said, "Hey, Tito, what's up?" I told him to hold up a minute and asked if he remembered seeing me at the Playboy Mansion the other night. He said, "Not really, but I was kind of fucked up." So I told him, "I like you. You're an awesome artist, but you were being disrespectful to my girl. You were hitting on her right in front of me. I think you need to apologize to her right now." He said, "Man, I'm sorry. I apologize. I was drunk." I walked him over to where Jenna was standing and he apologized to her.

After he left, Jenna looked at me and smiled. She said, "Nobody has ever done that for me."

JENNA JAMESON *I remembered telling Tito when we first started going out that he was going to end up getting into a lot of fights because people are always going to be disrespectful to me. But people will not be disrespectful to you.*

And then there was my little run-in with the band Maroon 5.

I was in New York doing some press and Jenna told me that while I was out she had received an e-mail from the singer from the group Maroon 5, saying that he wanted to get her number and that she should give him a call. Jenna said, "You don't have anything to worry about. I just wanted you to know."

I said, "Cool. Give me the guy's number."

I called the number and got his voice mail. I said, "What's up? This is Jenna Jameson's boyfriend, Tito Ortiz. If you want to talk to my girlfriend, you give me a call." I left my number and hung up. Jenna just looked at me, amazed. She said, "Are you serious? You just called him?"

I told her nobody is punking me. It just isn't happening.

The next day Jenna got a call from the band's manager, who bent over backward trying to smooth over the situation. He said that was not the intention of the call and that the band wanted her to appear in one of their videos. We both knew what he was saying was crap.

But Jenna realized at that moment that I loved her that much and that I would fight for her.

JENNA JAMESON *Then there was the night I was out and Tito was working. Criss Angel came up and started hitting on me. He was like, "Hey, baby, want to go for a ride in my Lamborghini?" I said I had my own Lamborghini and I walked away.*

Later that night, he found out that I was dating Tito and he came over to me and apologized. He said, "Please tell Tito that I didn't mean to hit on you and that I didn't realize that you and he were together." He was really groveling. He ended up calling Tito and leaving a message apologizing and asking for forgiveness. People are so intimidated by him and he's real good about keeping the wolves away from my door.

It was inevitable that I would eventually run into Jenna's ex-husband. That came about when Jenna and I went to the Adult Video News Convention in Las Vegas. Everybody knew that Jenna's ex was going to be there and the press immediately started predicting that he and I would get into it and that there would be this big violent brawl.

When we got there, I found out that Jenna's ex had actually hired security because he wanted to look like a bad dude when he walked into the convention hall. But that was his own doing. I don't think he was doing that because of me. There was no way I was going to beat him down.

JENNA JAMESON *I made sure Tito was with me at the convention. He's in my life and I wanted him to be there. But there was no reason for Tito and my ex-husband to come in contact. I never wanted Tito to have to deal with my ex-husband. So while we were in the convention hall, I made sure to steer Tito* *as far away from him as possible. It was all such a ridiculous drama, but I really didn't want them to meet.*

We did meet up later that night at a nightclub and we shook hands. We had no hostility toward each other. I sensed that he respected me and the kind of person I am, but the thing at the AVN convention was merely a matter of two guys sizing each other up. No lines were crossed, so there was no reason for me to get into it with him.

Being around Jenna and being in a long-term relationship with Kristin has caused me to think about my relationships with women over the years. I could never be without a woman in the past because I was always in dire need of someone to take care of me. But in past relationships I've always had this need to see if the grass was greener on the other side; even when I've been with women who didn't mean more to me than sex.

I've been lucky with two women. Kristin was never with me for my money. She loved me and took care of me. She was not in love with Tito Ortiz the fighter. She was in love with Jacob, who was a good kid and who was going to grow up and be a high school teacher. Jenna is the same way. She could care less about how much money I have and because of her I've stopped looking elsewhere.

Like a lot of stuff, my dealings with women stem from the abandonment issues I have because of the way my parents treated me when I was growing up. It took me years to come to grips with that stuff, and Jenna's been real helpful with that.

JENNA JAMESON *At the year mark in the relationship is when the challenges begin, and we've had a few bumps in the road. Tito is a very jealous guy. He wants to be number one at all times, and sometimes I think he needs to be reminded of that. There have been times when he felt that I was paying too much attention to somebody that I shouldn't have been paying attention to. That's been a constant. Tito's a sensitive guy and sometimes I don't take his feelings into consideration. He's had to remind me that now it's Jenna's and Tito's world and not just Jenna's world.*

For the past ten years I've had this recurring dream about waking up in a house and not knowing where I am. I would go to an old house that I used to live in and somebody else would be living there. One day I was talking to Jenna about the dream and she just came out and said, "You have abandonment issues." The problem isn't completely solved, but knowing why I behave the way I do has been half the battle for me.

Jenna spends a lot of time at my house but she has her own place as well. You won't see any paparazzi hanging around my place. I have no problem with them because they're intimidated by me. Because they don't know me and can only judge me by my image, they think I'm a loose cannon.

There are always a few paparazzi hanging out at Jenna's house. But when I show up they leave. When we go out, it's even crazier. They'll come up and snap a few shots, which is okay with me. But if they get too close, I'll give them a look and they'll just step back. Some of them are okay, but a lot of them are just a little too pushy.

When we go downtown to a restaurant or someplace public, it can get a little crazy. I'm kind of the alpha male dog in the room with a bunch of mutts. When I walk into a room with Jenna, people look at her, then they look at me and turn away.

But the real people, the people who are not somehow connected to the business, they're the funniest of all. They'll come up to me and ask if it's okay if they take a picture with Jenna. I think a lot of them assume I'm her bodyguard. When it comes to things like autographs, it's the other way around. I get the autograph requests more than Jenna because a lot of them feel that she will be offended if they bother her. But they will go up to Jenna and ask her permission for them to take a picture with me.

Women come up to us all the time now because they want to have threesomes with us. And there are still women who come on to me because they think I have a lot of money and that they can get their hands on it by being close to me.

Well, that shit never worked before and it's certainly not going to work now. It's kind of sad. Why would I want to be with them when I'm with somebody who is beautiful and smart and is not after me for my money? You tell me.

Then there are the haters. There have been a lot of those since Jenna and I got together. We get a lot of the really nasty and hateful stuff on the Internet. When people are real mean and nasty to me, I can deal with it. But when they say things about Jenna, that bothers me a lot. All you can do is ignore that stuff. In fact, during our last contract negotiations, Dana White made some remarks about Jenna not being very bright. All I can say to that is that Dana White is one of the dumbest people I know and that Jenna is one of the smartest.

I still haven't figured this all out yet. Being with Jenna is a whole different world for me. But I do know one thing.

And that's that I love her with all my heart.

CHAPTER SIXTEEN

Fight to the Finish

*R*andy Couture had held the UFC light heavyweight title since he beat me in 2003. It seemed a bit ironic that the person who would take the title from him was my friend Chuck Liddell.

It was inevitable that I would fight him and that I would get my title back. I was thirty-one years old at that time and I had been fighting for ten years. Liddell was one of the best fighters in the business, so I knew I would have my hands full. And I knew I would have to train very seriously.

I was back up in Big Bear training hard. I was working on perfecting every aspect of my game, and I felt that everything was coming together. Then fate stepped in once again.

The UFC wanted me to go to Florida to appear on the Latin ESPY awards show. I caught the flu on the way back and by the time I got back to Big Bear, I was in really bad shape. They ended up having to take me to the emergency room. It turns out I had a real bad case of dehydration that had been compounded by the flu. The doctors ended up pumping five bags' worth of IV fluids into me. I was out of action for six days and by the time I had recovered enough to train, there were only three weeks left before the fight.

I had lost a lot of weight and felt very light. But I still felt like I was going to win.

During the buildup to the Liddell fight, Dana White started bad-mouthing me to the press again. He painted this real shitty picture of me as being a money-grubbing sonofabitch. And again I was kind of caught in the middle of his hostility because of Chuck Liddell.

Don't get me wrong. Chuck has been a good friend and training partner for a long time. It's just that we both have different attitudes about what is good for the fighters. I'm a firm believer that all fighters should get as much as we can because it's our asses on the line when we step into the Octagon. My feeling has always been, "Let's *really* get paid to do this." But Chuck doesn't really care that much.

He's kind of a trailer park kid who likes to dress in thongs and shorts. In a way, he's kind of unsophisticated. He's happy to have a house in San Luis Obispo and a couple of cars, and that's all he wants. That's not me. I want to make sure that I'm getting paid for the rest of my life and that my family will continue to make money off my name long after I stop fighting.

So if wanting that is a negative, then I guess I'm a real shithead.

The fight, billed as UFC 66: Liddell vs Ortiz 2, was held in Las Vegas. I felt good about everything that night. The fans were cheering me on instead of booing me. They saw a different person. Now, all of a sudden, Liddell was being booed and he looked like the bad guy.

The first round I lost, pure and simple. I was trying a lot of leg kicks, but Chuck just came out swinging. He hit me with an overhand right that opened up a cut over my left eye. I was down. But somehow I survived that round. I came back a little bit in the second round with a couple of take- downs and a couple of good shots. I thought I was getting back in it. In the third round I got hit with some pretty good shots. The cut over my left eye opened up again. I thought I was defending myself, but all of a sudden the referee stepped in and stopped it.

The victory shirt I had picked out for that night was appropriate whether I won or lost that fight. Even in defeat I wore it proudly. It said: "Thanks . . . U.S. Troops For Fight- ing For Our Country."

I was disappointed with the loss. I really wanted that title back. But in a sense I really couldn't complain too much. I was still one of the biggest, if not *the* biggest, draw in the UFC for a nonchampion. Every time I fought, there were millions of pay-per-view buys. Every time some record is broken, my name is attached to it. Anybody who knows any- thing about the sport knows my name.

The relations between me and the UFC had become par- ticularly strained, mostly because of the things Dana White was saying about me and because of the constant pressures of signing contracts and such. Finally, things got so bad that we agreed to settle our differences in the ring.

It seemed like the perfect way to take care of the situation, and my hope was that some money could be made off of the event that would benefit some charities and people who really needed help. So the talks began. The idea was to stage the fight March 24, 2007, and, hopefully, to do some kind of pay-per-view and DVD combination to really bring in some money. But the negotiations never really seemed to go anywhere.

And then one day in April, I turned on the television and there was Dana White doing an interview on Spike TV, accusing me of failing to show up for the fight. And, of course, there was no opportunity for me to respond to him.

The reality was that there never was a contract to sign and I sure as hell was not going to risk getting into the Octagon without something in writing. When I had originally talked with Dana, we had discussed a 50/50 split of whatever money was made. He denied that conversation ever took place. I realized that without a written agreement it was his word against mine, but it pissed me off that anybody would think I might have pussed out of the fight with Dana. It hurt my image, and I don't know why the UFC would want to hurt the image of one of their biggest stars.

We went back and forth on this for a while, and at one point, Chuck Liddell got into it and started giving interviews about how Dana was right and that I was afraid to fight him. Chuck was basically being Dana White's puppet at that point, and I said so. I knew Chuck was a company man, but I was still disappointed in him.

I would have loved to fight Dana, but I wasn't about to fight without a contract. And there would have to be some kind of money involved that I would be quite happy to donate to charity. I would have liked nothing better than to beat Dana White's ass, but I had a living to make, and so it was on to the next fight.

Word was getting around Hollywood that I was actually a fighter who could act and so, even without an agent, offers from film and television people began to come in. In between training and doing whatever I had to do to make money, I managed to get small parts in three films.

One was this cop movie called *Venice Underground* about undercover cops fighting drug dealers in Venice Beach. I also had a small role in this romantic comedy called *The Dog Problem*. But the role I am proudest of up to this point was in a film I made in Iraq called *Valley of the Wolves*. I play this military officer who discovers mercenary American soldiers fighting in the Middle East. I won't ruin it for you and tell you what happens. But I will tell you that anybody who doubts that I can act should see that movie. When the movies were done, it was back to the Octagon and fight preparation.

And it seemed like every time I turned around, my contract had some involvement in the outcome of a fight. I had two more fights on my current contract. But you have to understand how the UFC mind-set works. In their eyes, if I lost my next fight, they'd be able to justify offering me less money on my next deal. My next opponent was going to be Rashad Evans. I knew going in that if I lost to Rashad, I was setting myself up for a horrible negotiation.

The Evans fight came about after the Chuck Liddell fight and I was concerned about the possibility of losing two fights in a row—what it would do to my status and reputation, that kind of stuff. I think the UFC was concerned as well because they gave me a choice of three fighters: Keith Jardine, Forrest Griffin, and Rashad Evans. Keith had already lost to Rashad, and I had already beaten Forrest Griffin. I didn't want an easy fight, so I went with Rashad.

But I knew I was going to beat Rashad. He knew I was going to beat him and the UFC knew I was going to beat him. And the UFC knew that once I beat him, they were going to have to pay me what I was worth.

Rashad was a tough fighter, an undefeated fighter. He came from a wrestling background, and his boxing skills had gotten a lot better.

Once the fight was announced, it didn't take long for the trash talking to start and, as expected, it got pretty intense and nasty.

Rashad immediately started talking some shit about me. Normally I have a thick skin about that stuff. I know it's all part of hyping a fight and putting asses in the seats. But he was being a bit over-the-top and was pushing some buttons.

So I decided that maybe we should meet.

I knew he was going to be at the UFC 69 matches so I thought I'd go down there, shake his hand, and give him some respect. I saw him, went over, put out my hand, and said, "You're a tough fighter. I wish you good luck in your training. But watch what you say."

He stood up. We were face-to-face. He said, "What do you mean, watch what I say? You're not my dad. I can say anything I want! You're a fucking washout, and I'm going to beat your fucking ass!"

I just looked at him and said, "I'm going to cave your fucking face in!"

It was game on. I took it personally and I was pissed off.

From that moment on I was willing to give as good as I got in the trash-talk department. At one point there was a picture of him on a website with a caption that read: "The first UFC woman fighter." When you clicked on the picture it said: "7/7/07, The first woman fighter: Rashad Evans." And then it said I was going to make Rashad Evans "my nappy-headed ho." THAT was my doing. Yeah, it was more than a little racist and it was the very thing that got Don Imus into a lot of trouble. But for me it was a joke, even though it was a calculating joke. Hell, I'm Mexican. I hear that kind of stuff all the time. My best friend in the business, Rampage, is black, and he thought it was a joke. It was about a person and not a race, so I didn't think there was anything wrong with it.

We're involved in one of the most barbaric sports you can possibly be involved in. We make a living by hitting each other in the face and bloodying each other up. We're always looking for an edge. And as far as I'm concerned, if it takes something like that to get inside his mind, I'm going to say it.

While I was training for the Rashad Evans fight, I made what was probably the biggest purchase I will ever make. I bought Oscar De La Hoya's house up in Big Bear, California, for $2.1 million. Jenna was with me the day the deal closed, and we were walking around the property. She asked me if I was happy. Yes, I was happy. But I was also in a whole other place.

All I could think of was that I used to be this punk kid in Huntington Beach who was sniffing glue and going nowhere. And now I had just laid out $2.1 million for this huge house. I just couldn't believe that it was happening to me. It was just crazy, plain crazy.

My fight with Rashad was not the main event of UFC 73: Stacked, and it was not even a title fight. But it was probably the biggest gate ever for a nonchampionship card. There were more than a 400,000 pay-per-view buys for that one. And I think everyone knew who people were laying their money down to see. We weren't the main event, but we were treated like the main event. And it turned out to be a real tough fight.

I went through my pre-fight ritual of crying. Then the Huntington Beach Bad Boy took over and I was not afraid.

People were going crazy when I entered the ring. My entrance music, "Mosh," which I was using for the sixth consecutive fight, was bumping. The fight was on.

From the opening bell, it went back and forth. I pretty

much dominated with kicks and takedowns. Near the end of the round Rashad hit me a few times and I got cut under my eye. But it was no problem. In the second round I was dominating again until Rashad went for a takedown and I grabbed hold of the fence to keep from going down and I received a warning from the referee. Later in the round I ended up grabbing the fence again and a point was deducted. The round ended even. If I hadn't grabbed the fence, I would have won it. Rashad came on strong in the final round, but I pretty much held my own.

The judges gave me the first round and Rashad the third. The second round was called even and the fight was called a draw. It was a good fight. The only injury I got was a fracture of one of my orbital sockets. It looked a lot worse than it was, and the important thing was that, just like my other injuries, it would heal.

There was an immediate call for a rematch.

I knew there would be.

But win, lose, or draw, the T-shirt I wore that night pretty much said it all.

"Bad Boy For Life."

CHAPTER SEVENTEEN

Star-Spangled War Stories

Yes, I do vote. So I guess that entitles me to have an opinion. Especially about things like war.

I'm not your typical celebrity who decides on a cause without thinking about it real carefully. I watch CNN and all the political programs. I've listened to what people have had to say. I've always been supportive of the troops. But it took me a while to decide how I felt about the war.

We've been at war in Iraq for five years, and people just don't see that. People are too busy with their nine-to-five jobs and their nine-to-five lives to realize that there are kids fighting and dying in Iraq. For the most part, the only reason they are there is because they come from poor places and the only way they can make money is to go to war.

It's become a political war. I'm not a political person, but it's not that difficult to read between the lines. I'm against the war. But I'm one hundred percent in support of the troops.

I've said so on a lot of my victory T-shirts. And I'd like to think I've shown it with my actions.

When the Marines snubbed Jenna, it never got in the way of my supporting the military. I knew that it wasn't the troops' doing. Jenna and I have done other things with the troops since that happened, and the response has been fantastic. Sure, 9/11 was the catalyst that got me to support the troops. But I guess we all need something to get us involved. I've given a lot of support to the military since 9/11—I've visited troops on their bases, gone to see people in hospitals. Any time the USO called, I was there.

The USO called midway through 2007 and wanted to know if I wanted to go to Iraq. Going to Iraq for a week to say hi to all these kids who had left their families to go fight for their country, sign some autographs, and take some pictures simply to let them know that people were in their corner was the least I could do.

I flew out of Los Angeles on July 28, 2007. We flew into Washington, D.C., and I was taken to Bethesda Hospital and Walter Reed Army Hospital, where I got an up-close look at the price these kids were paying for fighting in Iraq.

I saw guys who had had their arms and legs blown off. There were guys who had suffered permanent brain damage from shrapnel from exploding IEDs (improvised explosive devices). Some guys couldn't even speak. Seeing the support their parents were giving them was heartwarming, but seeing these kids who had a body part missing or who were all shrapnel-scarred was really heart-wrenching.

Bethesda was a reality check for me. I was like, *Holy shit! This is what's really going on in Iraq right now.* What I saw really hurt me badly.

Then I was taken to Walter Reed, where a lot of the wounded were going through therapy. There was this one guy who had been stabbed in the head. The blade had barely missed his frontal lobe. He was okay and he was waiting to go through therapy so that he could go back and fight with his guys again. He wanted to go back to war, and the army was willing to let him. He said, "I have fifteen guys who are my brothers, and I want to go back there and help them." I was thinking, *Wow! I'm going to Iraq tomorrow and this is what I'm going to see?*

A couple of my friends, Justin McCulley and Kenny Knoll, came with me. We flew into Kuwait and went to a camp to meet with the guys. I posed for pictures and just talked to them, and they were real stoked.

We flew to four other camps to visit the troops, then they put us on a DC-130 and flew us into Baghdad. I was wearing a flak jacket and a helmet. Suddenly it really seemed like a war zone. All I could think was, *Are we going to get shot at?*

The last night of the tour we flew into Camp Victory and there was some incoming fire. Maybe a half-dozen rounds, but they were a long ways away. Being there and seeing the smiles on the guys' faces really touched me. Then we went to a place called Tajif. They had lost a lot of soldiers in the past year and their morale was really down. I walked in, the guys noticed me, and they seemed kind of bummed. Justin and I talked to them for about an hour, and by the time we left they had smiles on their faces.

I learned a lot from that trip. And the main thing is that getting in the Octagon and fighting isn't shit compared to what those guys do out there. Our soldiers are walking around with M16s, living in a war zone whether they're eating, sleeping, or taking a shit. These guys are on the front line, and seeing them at war was something that I had never experienced before. It made a real impact on me.

What I do is a sport, a competition, and we abide by a certain set of rules. What they do is reality. Seeing our soldiers at war really scared the shit out of me.

Going to Iraq was the first time in the year that Jenna and I had been together that we had been apart for any length of time. And I missed her. While I was gone, Jenna had decided to have a breast reduction and when I got off the plane and saw her, I was pleasantly surprised.

I had a brand-new woman to play with.

The idea of giving back did not end with the troops. Not long after I returned from Iraq, I went to Arizona to do my second annual blood drive for United Blood Services. I was there to sign autographs and encourage people to donate blood. This year we collected more than four hundred pints of blood, twice what we did the previous year.

The idea of helping and giving back has always been with me. When I first started fighting I would sometimes give a percentage of my winnings to charity. Sadly that hasn't happened much lately because, well, I've got bills to pay. But I have a history of donating my time for a good cause.

In 2000, I began a series of Ultimate Training Center seminars. People would donate toys or money and were offered the chance to come and train with me. I still try to do those every once in a while.

I was involved in the Miracle on First Street, an annual toy giveaway sponsored by the Hollenbeck Youth Center in Los Angeles. I remember I was driving down the street with the boxer Fernando Vargas and I saw all these kids and parents standing in a long line. I turned to Fernando and said, "You want to hear something funny? I remember when I was young, my family and I would be standing in lines like these." I was really touched by the scene. Fernando and I pulled up and started handing out toys. Fernando left after a couple of hours, but I stayed until every last kid was taken care of.

But while I like to give back, occasionally the best intentions are messed up. After I fought Ken Shamrock the first time, I decided to start up a Tito Ortiz Foundation to help out underprivileged and inner-city kids. I went to this company called Foundation Makers to license the charity. We were going to create a website, and they were talking about a charity golf tournament. Basically they promised me the world. So I wrote them a check for ten grand, which, in those days, was a lot of money for me. Then all of a sudden I started hearing that they couldn't get this and that, that the original ten grand was for the license and paperwork, and that now they needed more money from me. When I refused to give them more money they said I had signed a contract and they were going to sue me. So I ended up getting burned.

But things like that have not stopped me from doing charity events when I can. Because it's always nice to look in the mirror at the end of the day and see that you helped somebody's life . . . even if only a little bit.

CHAPTER EIGHTEEN
The Future Starts Now

*A*m I a dangerous person?

      With the tragedy of wrestler Chris Benoit, that question gets asked a lot more than it used to. Here's my answer . . .

I am not a dangerous person. Sure, I've robbed houses and cars and sold drugs and gotten into a lot of fights. Early on, the fights were always about self-defense or protecting somebody who was a friend. But even in those days, it was never about deliberately setting out to hurt somebody. I never used a gun or a knife. I can be upset with a person, but I would never hurt someone in anger. If I even sensed that a situation like that might come up, I would just walk away. Or get real quiet.

It's not as if there has never been a perception that any time I show up at a situation there's going to be a brawl. Sure, some guys may think that, and that's because they're scared of me. But when I'm out and about, there will never be blows thrown. I have people to do that. I don't have to.

When I'm out with my friends, they watch my back. They know better than to let me get into situations. I've hired security a few times. That has a lot to do with the crowds and the people I'm sometimes around. There are people who are respectful fans who just want a picture or an autograph or to just shake my hand. But sometimes I run into people who think because they've seen my fights and read all the stories they can just come up to me and get in my face, touch me, and all that kind of shit. So yeah, sometimes I have security to step in. Sometimes all it takes is for me to raise my voice and tell them to step the fuck back!

I've had situations where I've been angry with both Kristin and Jenna. We would be discussing something and it would get uncomfortable for me, so I would just get quiet or get up and walk away. That's my way of avoiding anger.

I've been angry with the UFC sometimes. Well, not so much with the UFC as with Dana White. In those kinds of situations it's often difficult to get quiet and just walk away. But the way I get around that is to realize that it's all just business. These days I find it very difficult to even be in the same room with Dana White, let alone do any kind of business with him. So I've decided to go over his head and deal with the UFC owners.

In a sense I've been dealing with anger issues when it comes to my father. I've been walking away from him for years. The last time I talked to him was when my son was born. When I got him tickets to that fight in Vegas, I never even saw him or heard from him afterwards. It was like all the hurt was still there and I just didn't want to deal with it.

I've never made peace with him, but he's seventy-one now and there probably isn't much time left, so I'm thinking that I will now. Christmas will be coming up soon. Maybe that will be the time to do it. I think the issues I have with my father are something I'm going to have to face. He's never said he was sorry for what he put us through when we were growing up, and I don't really understand that. I suppose I can hate him as much as I want.

But he's still my dad.

JOYCE ROBLES *I can understand why Tito feels the way he does about his father. He's a broken man. I haven't seen him or had anything to do with him for a long time. He really hurt Tito, which is why I'm staying out of the middle of all that.*

Another father-son relationship I am going to have to address real soon is the one I have with my son Jacob. I'd like to think that it's very good. But at times it does seem distant and at times it just plain sucks.

I try to see him at least three times a month, but sometimes things happen and I can't see him as often. I would have loved to be the one to help him learn how to ride a bike. But right now, Kristin's sister's husband is helping him do that. Hearing that kind of stuff is hard because I would like to be doing those things with him.

But it's hard to be a full-time father and be there for the important things in his life when I'm not always around.

When he was younger, we could explain my not being around by telling him that I was away at work, which, a lot of the time, was true. We couldn't really explain how his parents had split up because he wouldn't have understood it. But now he's around other kids who are always talking about their dads, and all he knows is that his dad is not around a lot. Kristin and I have talked about how we're going to have to explain this to him, and I think it's going to happen soon.

Jacob has started to ask questions now that he's five. And I've been as honest with him as I can possibly be. I just tell him that his mother and I aren't in love anymore; that we're in love but not with each other like a mother and father should be. We haven't talked to him about how the marriage fell apart and how we used to argue a lot. I don't think he's ready to understand that part of it yet.

Sometimes he comes out to California to visit and we do things as a family, going to Disneyland and places like that with Jenna. To Jacob, Jenna is my girlfriend. At this point, he hasn't asked any more about her than that. But I'm sure that at some point he will.

Hopefully, by the time he starts asking those kinds of questions, I'll have the answers.

It's disappointing that, with my son, I haven't been able to avoid the same mistakes my parents made. It makes me feel sad. Because at the end of the day, I just want to make sure that my son is happy and not dysfunctional the way I was.

Professionally, things have not gone according to plan, which is pretty much the way they've always been. My rematch with Rashad Evans was scheduled for November 17, 2007, in Newark, New Jersey.

And the trash talk had already started. As always, the hype was about getting people interested in the fight. In a way it was kind of a joke. But it was also about getting in Rashad's head and getting him pissed off and out of his fight plan. So he talks his smack, I talk my smack, but in the end it all comes down to what happens in the ring.

Then there's the profanity. In case you haven't noticed, I use the F bomb a lot. As well as the S bomb and a whole lot of other bombs. But as I've gotten more businesslike, I've made an attempt to clean up my mouth a bit. Sometimes when I'm doing an interview I'll be so conscious of trying not to curse that I come across as being a little stiff. A lot of people have told me not to worry about that and to just be myself. But I guess I think of the kids and how it might be encouraging them to curse as well. I'm sure there's a compromise in all this somewhere.

Since the first Rashad Evans fight, I have been negotiating a new contract with the UFC. And it always seems like it's the same old story. I have an attorney, but Jenna and I are handling all my contract negotiations. She's a savvy businesswoman and an excellent adviser when it comes to business matters. But I'm the one who makes the final decision. I've been through the wringer so many times with the UFC, I know what's good and what's not.

I've been a top fighter for the UFC for ten years, and quite simply, I think it's time for the UFC to step up and pay me for those ten years. Since the Fertittas bought the company in 2000, we've always negotiated contracts based on how profitable the company was at that time. They would always give me a little bit more. And I always settled for that on the condition that when the UFC started making more money, I would get more money as well.

Well, guess what, folks. The UFC made $231 million last year. I fought four times over the life of my last contract, and I had a lot to do with them making that money. So it's time to pay up.

This time around I'm negotiating totally with the Fertitta brothers and bypassing Dana alogether. With the UFC owners it's just business. With Dana the whole issue of contracts has become too personal. Every time I ask for more money, he feels like I'm taking it out of his pocket. Well, my feeling is that I'm the one who's going into the Octagon and fighting. Dana isn't.

I'm not going to lie to you and tell you that I'm not making damned good money. With the up-front money and what I'm getting from pay-per-view, I'm making close to a million a fight. And that doesn't even take into account what I make in a year from my clothing line.

And that's a lot more than most people will see in their lifetimes. Which sounds good until you realize that I'm in the fifty-one-percent tax bracket, the highest tax bracket you can be in. But people don't see that. All they see is this guy who is making a million.

Basically I'm asking the UFC for the same things I've always asked for: more money up front and more pay-per-view. I've been making close to a million per fight since signing the previous contract, and now I am asking for an even million per fight. I don't think that is being unreasonable, seeing as the UFC makes approximately forty million per fight. So far the negotiating is going fairly smoothly. The owners of the UFC and I both want me to finish my career with the UFC.

But that hasn't stopped people from other organizations from calling me. I get the calls all the time these days. But as soon as I hear who they are, I stop them and tell them I can't talk to them because I'm right in the middle of negotiations with the UFC.

But whoever I sign with, it's going to come down to them giving me what I want.

I don't know how much longer I will be fighting. In a perfect world I would say maybe two or three more years and then I will be done with it and want to move on to other things. But I know it's not a perfect world, so four or five more years is probably a more realistic timetable.

My feeling is that I want to make as much money as I can over the next few years and then move up to the next level. I'd like to be able to retire at age forty-five, and I think that's possible. My clothing line has been doing real well for a long time. And I'm getting more and more acting opportunities.

I would like to be an action movie star, and I've had a couple of people tell me that I have the potential to be the next Vin Diesel. I know acting would not be easy; it involves a lot of hard work and it's a difficult business. But in a way it's just like fighting. I was a champion because of hard work and dedication. Being an actor is certainly possible if I just focus and get it done.

And people recognize that I might just have what it takes to make it as an actor. Early in 2007, I appeared in a small role in an episode of the TV series *Numb3rs*. I also did a cameo in a movie that Jenna was in called *Zombie Strippers*. It was cool being on the set and watching Jenna work. As always, she was all business. As always, I was impressed.

I'm starting to see how Hollywood works. Your name gets mentioned as somebody who might be good for a project. Sometimes you get a call. Sometimes it turns out to be just smoke and mirrors. But I've been happy with the way my acting career is going and I'm ready for whatever comes next.

But before any of that acting stuff happens, I would like to get the championship back one more time. And that isn't going to be as easy as simply training like a demon for six months and then just beating the shit out of the other guy.

The current UFC lightweight champion is Quinton "Rampage" Jackson, who is not only a very good fighter but also a good friend of mine, probably one of the closest friends I've made in the fight game. We've been training together for nearly ten years. If it happens, it's going to be hard to fight somebody I'm friends with. We'll do the usual trash talking and all that and then, come the night of the fight, we'll stand in the center of the ring and probably bust out laughing. I think it will be exciting if we ever do challenge one another. And I'm sure it will be one hell of a fight.

But if we end up making two to three million for the fight, I know I can put aside our friendship for fifteen minutes. I would never try to take the food out of his son's mouths or make him incapable of earning a living as a fighter.

So I'll try not to hurt him too bad.

But I think a lot of people will pay a lot of money to see two old friends fight.

Writing this book has been so therapeutic for me in so many ways. It's forced me to relive a lot of stuff for better or worse. The other day I was sitting with Jenna and all of a sudden I just busted out laughing. She wanted to know what was so funny. I told her I was just thinking about a lot of the crazy shit I had been through.

But one thing changed for me during the writing process that was totally unexpected.

I've stopped smoking pot. I know what you're thinking. *He started out saying that he still used pot recreationally.* And I did. I would smoke pot on occasion during the writing of this book.

But one day, after a long writing session, I started to think about what my life has been about and where it's going. I just decided that if I was going to be a professional, clearheaded businessman in dealing with whatever comes my way in the future, I would have to give it up. So that day, I smoked one last joint.

And then I was done.

How the Story Ends

*T*here's always something going on in my life. If I tried to make this book totally up-to-date, the book would never come out. At some point I just have to say enough is enough.

So it's finally time to close the door.

I just got back from New York, where I filmed the television series *Celebrity Apprentice*. It aired in January, so you all know how it turned out and how I did. It was a good opportunity to learn a lot about business, plus being on a prime-time network television series didn't hurt my profile.

I accepted the *Celebrity Apprentice* gig at a time when circumstances beyond my control caused me to step back and just think about things. Circumstances that began with my having to back out of the Rashad Evans rematch.

I had been having recurring back problems for quite a while, and it finally boiled down to my wanting to be one hundred percent healthy before I competed again. I wasn't going to fight at seventy percent and make some other fighter look good, so I called up the UFC and told them I wasn't in any condition to fight. I'm sure you heard a lot of stories and smack going down about my pulling out of the fight. But the reality was that, physically, I was in no condition to fight.

The UFC is trying to set up a fight for me in February 2008. At this point I wouldn't mind fighting Shogun or any other top-five fighter. It's typical of the UFC not to let me know who I'll be fighting until the last six weeks. So my opponent is still a mystery to me at the time of this writing.

But if and when I have my next fight, that will be the last fight on my current contract. Because as of mid-November 2007, talks with the UFC have broken down. We've been going back and forth for a while but, all of a sudden, I haven't heard from them in weeks. You know how it goes. It's what I want versus what they want to give me. And right now, that's the big stumbling block.

If the UFC is making twenty million per fight, I want a big chunk of that. My feeling is that when I start making twenty-five to fifty percent of the gate, that's when it will all start to make sense.

I've got about three more years left as a fighter. I don't want to look back later and think, *Damn! I should have taken advantage of my last few years of competition in every possible way.*

A couple of months ago, I was invited to Washington, D.C., by the USO to present an award to a soldier at this big gala dinner. While we were in Washington, I went on a tour of the Capitol Building with Jenna. We were led around by Senator Arlen Specter, which was totally cool. We got to sit in on one of the congressional sessions and I got to see things like the Declaration of Independence and the Bill of Rights. I was seeing things from our country's history that I had only ever seen in books. It was a totally amazing experience for me.

There. You're pretty much caught up on my life. And we're at the end of the book. I've wanted to write this book for years. I wanted to let people know that it is possible for somebody to start out living a life as a total zero and end up living a life that most people dream about. It's a happy ending . . . hell, it's a great ending. But I'm only thirty-two. Getting to this point only makes me want to survive and to work even harder. I'm stoked to have been able to tell my story.

I'm still standing. There's more to come.

—Tito Ortiz, November 2007

The Dossier

NAME: Jacob "Tito" Ortiz
NICKNAME: The Huntington Beach Bad Boy
BORN: January 23, 1975
HEIGHT: 6 ft. 2 in.
WEIGHT: 205 lbs.
TEAM ASSOCIATION: Team Punishment
FIGHTING STYLE: Wrestling, Submission Wrestling, Muay Thai

MMA FIGHTING RECORD

15 Wins
8 by Knockout
2 by Submission
5 by Decision
5 Losses
1 Draw

T-SHIRTS

UFC 18, Jerry Bohlander: I Just Fucked Your Ass
UFC 19, Guy Mezger: Gay Mezger Is My Bitch

UFC 22, Frank Shamrock: Tito put on a Frank Shamrock T-shirt and had Shamrock sign it.

UFC 25, Wanderlei Silva: I Just Killed The Axe Murderer!

UFC 29, Yuki Kondo: RESPECT I don't earn it I just fucken take it

UFC 30, Evan Tanner: If You Can Read This I Just Stomped His Ass!

UFC 32, Elvis Sinosic: That's American For "Whoop Ass" Mate

UFC 33, Vladmir Matyushenko: Fighting For America

UFC 40, Ken Shamrock: I Just Killed Kenny! You Bastard!

UFC 50, Patrick Côté: Who's Next!

UFC 51, Vitor Belfort: Bring Home Our Troops!

UFC 59, Forrest Griffin: With Great Sacrifice Comes Great Rewards

UFC 61, Ken Shamrock: If You Fight Tito Ortiz You Lose!

Ortiz vs Shamrock 3, Ken Shamrock: Punishing Him Into Retirement

UFC 66, Chuck Liddell: Thanks . . . U.S. Troops For Fighting For Our Country

UFC 73, Rashad Evans: Bad Boy For Life

ENTRANCE MUSIC
UFC 30: "Rollin'," Limp Bizkit
UFC 32: "Break Stuff," Limp Bizkit
UFC 33: "Break Stuff," Limp Bizkit
UFC 40: "Break Stuff," Limp Bizkit

UFC 44: "Let's Do This Now," KoRn

UFC 47: "Bad Boy For Life," P. Diddy

UFC 50: "Bad Boy For Life," P. Diddy

UFC 51: "Mosh," Eminem

UFC 59: "Mosh," Eminem

UFC 61: "Mosh," Eminem

Ortiz vs Shamrock 3: "Mosh," Eminem

UFC 66: "Mosh," Eminem

UFC 73: "Mosh," Eminem

PROFESSIONAL FIGHTING CAREER

UFC 13 vs Wes Albritton: Win: TKO (strikes), May 30, 1997, Augusta, Georgia

UFC 13 vs Guy Mezger: Loss: Submission (Guillotine Choke), May 30, 1997, Augusta, Georgia

West Coast NHB vs Jeremy Screeton: Win: Submission (Strikes), December 8, 1998

UFC 18 vs Jerry Bohlander: Win: Decision, January 8, 1999, New Orleans, Louisiana

UFC 19 vs Guy Mezger: Win: TKO (Strikes), March 3, 1999, Bay St. Louis, Mississippi

UFC 22 vs Frank Shamrock: Loss: Submission (Strikes), September 24, 1999, Lake Charles, Louisiana

UFC 25 vs Wanderlei Silva: Win: Decision, April 14, 2000, Tokyo, Japan

UFC 29 vs Yuki Kondo: Win: Submission (Neck Crank), December 16, 2000, Tokyo, Japan

UFC 30 vs Evan Tanner: Win: KO (Slams), February 23, 2001, Atlantic City, New Jersey

UFC 32 vs Elvis Sinosic: Win: TKO (Cut), June 29, 2001, East Rutherford, New Jersey

UFC 33 vs Vladimir Matyushenko: Win: Decision, September 28, 2001, Las Vegas, Nevada

UFC 40 vs Ken Shamrock: Win: TKO (Corner Stoppage), November 22, 2002, Las Vegas, Nevada

UFC 44 vs Randy Couture: Loss: Decision, September 26, 2003, Las Vegas, Nevada

UFC 47 vs Chuck Liddell: Loss: KO (Punches), April 2, 2004, Las Vegas, Nevada

UFC 50 vs Patrick Côté: Win: Decision, October 22, 2004, Atlantic City, New Jersey

UFC 51 vs Vitor Belfort: Win: Decision, February 6, 2005, Las Vegas, Nevada

UFC 59 vs Forrest Griffin: Win: Decision, April 15, 2006, Anaheim, California

UFC 61 vs Ken Shamrock: Win (Strikes), July 8, 2006, Las Vegas, Nevada

Ortiz vs Shamrock 3 vs Ken Shamrock: Win: TKO (Punches), October 10, 2006, Hollywood, Florida

UFC 66 vs Chuck Liddell: Loss: TKO (Punches), December 30, 2006, Las Vegas, Nevada

UFC 73 vs Rashad Evans: Draw, July 7, 2007, Sacramento, California

Acknowledgments

I want to thank these people for their love, encouragement, and friendship. Without them my life would be a much emptier place. My mother Joyce. My father Samuel. My brothers Jim and Marty. Kristin Ortiz, Jenna Jameson, Paul Herrera, Raul Duarte, Scott Rotherd, the Nicely family, the Rotherd family, Wayne Harriman, and Keith Harriman. Love to you all.